FIRST NATIONS
—*Firsthand*

FIRST NATIONS
—*Firsthand*

A history of five hundred years of encounter, war, and peace inspired by the eyewitnesses

CAMERON FLEET, *Editor*

CHARTWELL
BOOKS, INC.

Page 2 photograph: Placating the Spirit of a Slain Eagle, by Edward S. Curtis.

Above: An Ojibwa woman and child on Garson Lake, Saskatchewan.

Published by
CHARTWELL BOOKS, INC.
A division of BOOK SALES, INC.
114, Northfield Avenue
Edison, New Jersey 08837

Produced by
Saraband Inc, PO Box 0032, Rowayton, CT
06853-0032

Copyright © 1997, Saraband Inc.

Design © Ziga Design

ISBN 0-7858-0680-6

Printed in China

10 9 8 7 6 5 4 3 2 1

EDITOR: Cameron Fleet
CONTRIBUTING EDITORS: Spencer Hart, Diana Steer Holdsworth
PROJECT CONSULTANT: Lynne Arany
ASSOCIATE EDITOR: Barbara Paulding Thrasher
EDITORIAL ASSISTANT: Nicola Gillies

Contents

Introduction

*"All children of Earth will be welcome
at our council fires."*

—SENECA PROVERB

Before the Europeans came, people lived in the Americas for thousands of years. They spoke diverse languages and developed cultures attuned to the nature of their lands, whether desert, plain, woodland, or arctic wilderness. Their life skills became traditions, each generation passing them on to the next, acknowledging the wisdom of their elders.

For most traditional peoples, time, as conceived by the majority, does not exist. The seasons flow in a great circle, repeated again and again. Customs outlive knowledge of their origins and are elevated to the sacred; reverence for them influences social behavior, and there is no need for laws to be written down and argued over. In pre-contact North America, youngsters were generally treated with indulgence by all members of the community: thus they were naturally disposed to take care of others in return. Trained from youth to place the tribe above individual concerns, all knew that the tribe would take care of them.

New World Civilizations

At contact, most of the New World's people lived as hunter-gatherers, as seminomads like the tribes of the Great Plains, or as efficient farmers like the Pueblo dwellers of the Southwest. However simple their lifeways appeared, the various cultures were rich in ceremony and ritual, their social organization was complex, their skills and crafts effective and impressive. In a few cases, the Americas brought forth highly developed civilizations, including the Inca of what is now Peru and the Maya and Aztec of present-day Mexico. In their time, they were among the world's most advanced.

The Inca built sophisticated roads that connected a centrally organized empire. Their experiments with horticulture led to the development of more than 300 kinds of potato, ensuring that this vital food could be grown in all seasons, climates, and altitudes. In the ninth century AD, at the height of the Maya culture, its scientific knowledge rivaled that of any society in the world. Mayans produced magnificent ceremonial cities and pyramids, a form of mathematics that included the concept of zero, a calendar system that remains unsurpassed, and hieroglyphic writing, to say nothing of fine sculpture, painting, and ceramics.

Native Americans also entertained visitors from abroad. Around AD 1000, native peoples, possibly Inuit, met Vikings in what is now Newfoundland. They attempted to trade their skins for Viking weaponry, but were refused. Instead, the Vikings proffered milk from the cows they had brought—a novelty to their hosts—and admired the skin boats the natives paddled with such dexterity. Although the Vikings returned to Greenland, one of their parties may have traveled into the interior as far as Minnesota, where Lakota Sioux say they intermarried with their ancestors. Other legends—whether historically grounded or not—tell of early contact with several different foreign visitors, including Egyptian explorers who reached southern shores, and European fishermen who landed in the Northeast. Columbus, then, was far from the first "discoverer" of the Americas.

Opposite: An ancient tradition and remarkable skill: spearing salmon in a Northwestern river.

Right: *A European depiction of a Southeastern tribesman with man-size bow, reed quiver, loincloth, body paint, and bead and feather ornaments.*

West Meets East

In the Americas, the Spanish were the first conquistadors, but not the last. When the English, French, and other Europeans saw the Spanish amassing great wealth from the gold and silver mines of Mexico, it was not long before they set about building their own empires. Over the next five hundred years, relations between native Americans and the newcomers would follow a tragic pattern. This was the case whether the Europeans were French, Spanish, or English, the natives who met them Taino, Aztec, or Chumash.

At first, natives would greet their visitors with the hospitality they were accustomed to offering any newcomer. Naturally, they expected to be met on the same terms. However, the Europeans returned the favor only as necessary to gain a foothold. Soon they were making and breaking treaties at will, lying without compunction, killing, and stealing land and possessions.

Although native Americans fought back, several factors worked against them from the start. The first was not the lack of suitable weaponry, as one might expect, but disease transported from the Old World, to which they had little resistance. All across the continent, people who had never laid eyes on a white man would soon die of smallpox or measles.

According to a 1969 study by historians Woodrow Borah and Sherburne F. Cook, *Conquest and Population: A Demographic Approach to Mexican History,* less than a century after Spanish conquest, the population of central Mexico had shrunk from 25 million to under 2 million. Borah and Cook suggest that had this drastic decline not occurred, the history of Mexico might have been more like that of China or India: foreign rulers could have been expelled by a numerically superior native society. The demographics of peoples north of the Rio Grande has not been

> ### *"The landscape is our church, a cathedral. It is like a sacred building to us."*
>
> —Zuni saying

studied as thoroughly, but historians including Francis Jennings have proposed that the successive plagues that spread across the hemisphere probably caused a population decline similar to that which occurred in Mexico. By 1600, according to their calculations, less than a tenth of the original population remained. It was mainly for this reason that Europeans quickly gained control.

Second, the Indian view of warfare differed from the European: it was more like a rigorous sport than an all-out effort to destroy. Native men, in effect, clashed with those of other tribes mainly to defend hunting territories; few "wars" of policy or ideology were conducted. But the Spanish, fresh from their 700-year conflict with the Moors, had developed an effective and deadly war machine. So had the other Europeans who followed them.

Third, most native people had a radically different view of leadership than did the newcomers. Among the Indians, chiefs were chosen to lead by example in peace and war—by moral authority, not by force. If they proved unworthy or ineffective, they were replaced or ignored. While this gave people much individual freedom, it also made them inexperienced in banding together against a common foe. Attempts to form coalitions against the invaders, led by Pontiac, Tecumseh, and others, were exceptions to the rule and largely unsuccessful.

The behavior of the Europeans, which appears so outrageous today, stemmed from several sources, not the least of which was greed. But at its most radical, this behavior was perceived as spiritually motivated.

Gardeners In Paradise
As their origin myths and religious traditions show, Europeans and native Americans could hardly have viewed life more differently. Thus they treated the Earth and each other in rad-

ically different ways. Most native Americans believed that creation is a continuous process, and that humans are placed on Earth in part to re-create the Great Mystery's (or Creator's) works—to be co-creators. Indigenous people saw the Earth as the great mother, the source of all life, the protector, the womb whence all came and to whom all would return to begin life anew.

Elements of many native origin stories are seen in that of the Iroquois, the Northeastern confederacy that includes the Mohawk, Oneida, Onondaga, Cayuga, and Seneca:

In the beginning, people lived beyond the sky, because deep waters covered the entire earth. Then, a pregnant woman fell from the Sky World toward the water. Ducks and geese broke her fall with their wings and carried her to the Great Turtle, master of all animals, and set her on his back. The Turtle ordered the other animals to bring earth

Below: *An early Spanish map of Aztec Mexico City (Tenochtitlán), which rose from the swamps of Lake Texcoc to dominate Middle America during the fifteenth century. When Cortés arrived, it was larger than any European city except London.*

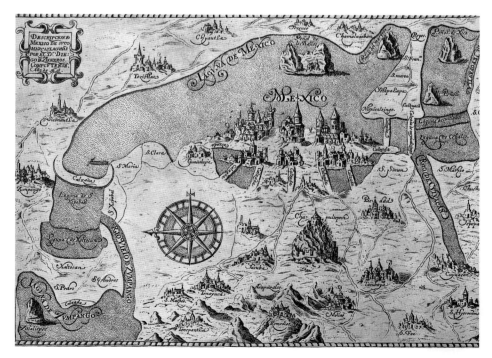

from the bottom of the water and cover his back that she might have land to live upon. When this magic earth was on his back, the woman was told to dance upon it in a sun-wise circle, and as she did, Great Turtle began to grow into a large island—North America. Eventually, the woman gave birth to a daughter who gave birth to twin sons.
—*Iroquois Creation Story*

Below: *A Plains encampment during the migratory summer hunt for the buffalo. The Sun Dance, a major ritual, was performed at the summer solstice.*

Opposite: *An Edward Curtis photograph from 1908,* The Berry Gatherers. *Curtis left an invaluable record of life among the tribes west of the Mississippi at the turn of the century. He became deeply fascinated with their lifeways and spent thirty years documenting their cultures.*

Father Sun's warming rays penetrated Mother Earth, engendering life from her fertility. Native peoples did not so much "worship" the sun as appreciate the forces, the powers, behind it, as they revered the forces behind all of creation, the spiritual powers in every rock and tree. For them, everything, including the Earth itself, was alive.

The Europeans perceived nature very differently. Like other modern people, they regard almost everything else in nature as inanimate. Even today, many believe, for example, that "animals have no feelings," certainly no souls. To native Americans, it was clear that they did. They felt no guilt in the act of killing to live, but showed responsibility by honoring the animals they hunted, accepting by ritual what they saw as the animal's deliberate sacrifice on their behalf. Part of one's responsibility was to ensure in this way that animal or vegetable spirits would remain benevolent, providing more food when the tribe required it.

> ## "*Before eating, always take a little time to thank the food.*"
> —ARAPAHO PROVERB

In the early 1930s, Yale University ethnographer Cornelius Osgood lived among the Alaskan Peel River Gwich'in. He described the difference in perception between Native and Western by writing: "It is as though one were to walk through a field of tall grass, and suddenly discover that his eyes had deceived him, that each blade waving in the wind was a snake." Writing in the early 1900s, Diamond Jennes, a Canadian who lived with subarctic peoples, made similar observations: "The

> *"Brothers, since these Englishmen have seized our country, they have cut down the grass with scythes, and the trees with axes."*
>
> —MIANTONOMI, NARRAGANSETT, 1642

Below: Native American "idols" are smashed by zealous Europeans in an engraving from the 1626 Narrative of Jean Bossus.

Indians believed that a stump could momentarily change to a man, that the caribou could push back the hood from its face and gaze out of a human countenance, that the snake or the owl could address the sleeping Indian in his own tongue."

The world was alive and awaited the involvement and interaction of man at every level of existence, spiritual, emotional, and physical. Europeans, however, had learned to fear nature, to set themselves up in opposition to it, to look to an alternative in heaven for any true reward:

The white man does not understand the Indian for the reason that he does not understand America. He is too far removed from its formative processes. The roots of the tree of his life have not yet grasped the rock and soil. The white man is still troubled with primitive fears; he still has in his consciousness the perils of this frontier continent, some of its vastness not yet having yielded to his questing footsteps and inquiring eyes.… But in the Indian the spirit of the land is still vested.
—Luther Standing Bear, Oglala Lakota

Land of the Spotted Eagle

What the newcomers seemed to fear most, besides the natives themselves, was the forest. It had taken millennia for the forests of North America to mantle vast areas of the continent. Over the centuries, native people had done little to affect them adversely. Legend held that before the white man, a squirrel could travel through the branches from the Atlantic to the Mississippi and never set paw to ground.

But the settlers began cutting down the ancient forest immediately, clearing it first for small homesteads, then for huge plantations. Dissenting voices were few. In the eighteenth century, Quaker John Woolman, an early ecologist, complained of the unnecessary destruction of timber. If people took only what they needed, he advised, they wouldn't have to keep encroaching on native holdings. In his nineteenth-century tour of America, Charles Dickens expressed horror at the sight of rotting stumps and torn earth, and advised his American fans to give the country back to the Indians.

Native Americans observed that of all creatures, man was the weakest. Humans had neither claws to scratch with, nor eagle eyes to see for miles, nor swift legs to run like the deer. They learned to survive by observing the habits of the animals they hunted and encountered, praying to acquire their strength, cleverness, and heightened sensitivities. The one great strength that humans did possess, and their purpose in life, was to care for the Earth in spiritual ways. It was their duty to pray for the Earth and all its creatures. If everything remained in balance, if all creatures took only what they needed and made the necessary sacrifices, then all would have enough to eat, and all, including the tribe, would live. In this world view, humans could be described as gardeners in paradise.

Rejected from the Garden

The Europeans who conquered the New World had a very different spiritual background. The Judeo-Christian religious tradition taught that there were not many powers—as the natives' living Earth, sun, animal, and insect—but only one God, perceived as all-powerful and easily angered. Man, having been expelled from paradise by an exacting God who resented independent thinking or behavior, was forced to live on a difficult and dangerous Earth. The only hope of escape from its pain and misery was through restraining his natural impulses to reach a heaven reopened by the sufferings and resurrection of Christ.

"If this is the way they pray, that is, bullets through people's hearts, I hope they will not pray for me."

—WILLIAM APESS, PEQUOT

Above: *Gathering fruit from the gigantic saguaro cactus of the Southwest, used as a source of food, fuel, and framing for shelters.*

The first man had angered God by listening to woman, who tempted him to eat from the tree of knowledge of good and evil. Woman, having shown her inherent weakness by succumbing to the blandishments of an evil power disguised as a snake, was considered unstable. Children, born of sinful man and woman, had to be disciplined into goodness. Although child-rearing practices varied to some extent among the Europeans, the general view was that sparing the rod meant spoiling the child. Later, when native children were taught by European missionaries, the same harsh principles were applied to them. The Christianized European could not enjoy life or nature on nature's terms, as the native American did. He saw himself as a spiritual exile, condemned "to earn his bread by the sweat of his brow." His orientation was toward an inhospitable world that it was his God-given duty to claim and subdue. The cultural concomitants of this world view included hierarchical societies in which discipline and obedience made members easier to control. This enhanced cooperation in such enterprises as waging war and amassing material goods.

Small wonder that most Europeans, trained to manage and control, viewed native attachment to uncultivated land as perverse, native reluctance to "modernize" as ignorant, native dislike of hard work to no apparent purpose as lazy, and native love for nature as more proof of childish inferiority. By so dehumanizing natives, Europeans could rationalize dealing with them harshly. Thus the violent interactions between Europeans and natives could have been predicted. It is to the credit of humanity that through it all, friendships were formed, marriages made, and true understanding begun.

The Return of the White Brother

A recurring prophecy among peoples of North, Central, and South America was the coming of the white man. The Aztec leader Montezuma (or Moctezuma) was terrified by the arrival of Hernán Cortés in the early sixteenth century. Montezuma believed him to be the god Quetzalcoatl, foretold by the prophecies. Years before any white man was seen in the north, native elders, enlightened by dreams, told their people that a day was coming when strange men with hair on their faces and skin like ghosts would appear from across the waters. In most accounts, the coming of the white man presaged the end of the world.

Ancient Hopi prophecies had a similar theme. Two brothers, one red, the other white, once lived together on Turtle Island (North America). One day the white brother left to discover new worlds and make new inventions, leaving his red brother to grow corn and to pray, in the traditional way. One day, the white brother would return, and the priests would know by certain signs whether he had remembered the spiritual instructions of the Creator—whether he had remained good. If the white brother appeared among them holding a cross within a circle, a Golden Age would begin upon Earth. But if he had forgotten the teachings and become evil, there would be no circle around the cross. When the Hopi saw their first Spanish friars, they knew that evil days lay ahead.

Below: A council of Plains people smoking the ritual feathered pipe known as the calumet, an emblem of peace.

Like many other peoples, the Hopi also had flood stories, whereby a world of evildoers was destroyed to initiate a new age. They believed that humans were now living in the fourth such world. In the first three, people had forgotten their spiritual heritage to become egotistical and destructive, at which point they were destroyed in cataclysms of fire or water. Life on earth had begun anew.

Hopi prophecies, like those of others in this hemisphere, hold that we are now living in such an end time. We have but a few years before the "purification" of Earth recurs, and she cleanses herself of despiritualized human life through earthquake, flood, and fire. The Hopi believe that this fourth world is the last—that we humans will not be given another chance.

The following chapters may be said to describe the return of the white brother before he understood the consequences of his inventions and the cost of forgetting spiritual values. In the light of today's ecology movements, and radical changes in consciousness regarding Earth and North America's first people, perhaps the good white brother is returning at last.

My great-grandfather [Nanámakee] was born in the vicinity of Montreal, where the Great Spirit first placed the Sauk Nation, and inspired him with a belief that, at the end of four years, he should see a white man, who would be to him a father. Consequently he blacked his face, and ate but once a day (just as the sun was going down) for three years, and continued dreaming throughout all this time whenever he slept—when the Great Spirit again appeared to him, and told him that at the end of one year more, he should meet his father—and directed him to start seven days before its expiration and take with him his two brothers, Namah, or Sturgeon, and Paukahummawa, or Sun Fish, and travel in a direction to the left of sun-rising. After pursuing this course five days, he sent out his two brothers to listen if they could hear a noise, and if so, to fasten some grass to the end of a pole, erect it, pointing in the direction of the sound, and then return to him.

Early next morning they returned, and reported that they had heard sounds which appeared near at hand, and that they had fulfilled his order. They all then started for the place where the pole had been erected; when, on reaching it, Nanàmakee left his party, and went alone to the place from whence the sounds proceeded, and found that the white man had arrived and pitched his tent.

—Black Hawk, Sauk
Autobiography, *1833*

Above: *An Inuit woman in traditional clothing, with beadwork face ornaments. Tattoos and body piercing are marks of beauty and status among Arctic and Subarctic peoples.*

Arrival and Encounter

The Spanish were the first Europeans to undertake invasion, conquest, and colonization of the Americas on a large scale. Spain's considerable military expertise had been developed during protracted wars both on home ground, with the Moors, and abroad. Most notably, Spain had joined other European Christian powers in the crusades of the eleventh to thirteenth centuries against Muslim Turks for control of the Holy Land. The pronounced religiosity of the Spanish, in evidence since the period of the crusades, strongly contributed to their dismissive, intolerant attitude toward other cultures. Seeking, by the fifteenth century, new lands to conquer, they justified the means and ends of their quests in terms of the interests of the Church—by definition, any action was right and honorable if conducted for the furtherance of those interests.

Not long after Christopher Columbus came upon Caribbean islands for the first time, Spanish galleons would return with innumerable stolen treasures. Between 1500 and 1650, the weight of their haul of gold alone has been estimated at 200 tons. The effect of this vast influx of valuable goods would change Europe, and the world, forever.

The Earliest "Discoveries"

In 1492, Cristoforo Colombo of Genoa, Italy, better known as Christopher Columbus, set out with the backing of Spain's King Ferdinand and Queen Isabella to find a short, safe, and profitable route to Asia. The ostensible purpose of his expedition was to open an ocean link that would bypass the Turkish-controlled Middle East region—hostile territory since the crusades—for direct, unintercepted trade with the Orient. Columbus had studied navigation in Lisbon and participated in Portuguese voyages to the Azores and Africa, experiences that made him an accomplished seaman and that left him with no desire to attempt further exploration of African waters. Confident that a western course would bring him to the source of the East's exotic spices and silks, his 1492 expedition eventually brought him instead to the Bahama islands of the Caribbean, where he believed himself somewhere off the coast of coveted Asia. Before venturing beyond the white coral beach of the island, it is popularly believed, he knelt and christened his "discovery" San Salvador, in grat-

Opposite: King Ferdinand of Spain directs his attention across the Atlantic to San Salvador, the island recently "acquired" for him by Columbus, in this 1493 engraving.

Left: Christopher Columbus— the man given all the credit, and blame, for changing the course of history.

> "*Neither better people nor land can there be!*"
> —CHRISTOPHER COLUMBUS, 1492

Right: *The* Santa Maria, *one of the three ships that accompanied Columbus on his voyage to the New World, was shipwrecked in December 1492, two months after the landing on San Salvador. Columbus and his crew survived to undertake four more voyages across the Atlantic.*

itude for his good fortune. He took "possession [of the islands] in Your Highnesses' name, by royal crier and with Your Highnesses' royal banner unfurled, and it was not contradicted."

His journal on the fateful day of his landing on the island reads:

FRIDAY, 12TH OF OCTOBER. We arrived at a small island.... Presently we saw people. They go as naked as when their mothers bore them, and so do the women, although I did not see more than one young girl. All I saw were youths, none more than thirty years of age. They are very well made, with very handsome bodies, and very good countenances. Their hair is short and coarse, almost like the hairs of a horse's tail,...they wear [their hair] long and never cut it. They

paint themselves black, and they are the color of the [people of the Canary Islands], neither black nor white. Some paint their faces, others the whole body, some only round the eyes, others only on the nose. They neither carry nor know anything of arms, for I showed them swords, and they took them by the blade and cut themselves through ignorance. They should be good servants and intelligent, for I observed that they quickly took in what was said to them, and I believe they would easily be made Christians, as it appeared to me that they had no religion. I, our Lord being pleased, will take hence, at the time of my departure, six natives for your Highnesses, that they may learn to speak.

It is obvious from Columbus's writings that he was thrilled by the adventure of exploring uncharted waters, but also that after the new route itself, wealth, and specifically gold, was uppermost in his mind; he would find little of it before his fourth voyage, in 1502. Nevertheless, in a letter to his sponsor sovereigns of March 4, 1493, reporting on the first expedition, he announced his hope of bringing home "as much gold as you need, spicery of a certain pepper, and...so many slaves that they are innumerable; and they will come from the idolaters. All this I found on this hasty trip." He concluded that "all of Christendom should

Right: *Columbus claiming San Salvador with "Your Highnesses' royal banner unfurled," as he reported to his sponsors. The natives, he told them, "are fit to be ordered about and made to work."*

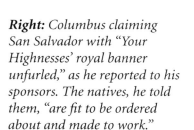

hold great celebrations, and especially God's Church," for the "friendly peoples" he had found, and their lands and goods.

In 1496, England's Henry VII, as staunch a member of the Catholic faith as were the rulers of Spain, commissioned John Cabot to "conquer, occupy, and possess" the lands of "heathens and infidels." Getting to the point, the king avoided Spanish-style religious directives to convert the heathen and simply ordered Cabot to get the "dominion, title and jurisdiction of the same."

John Cabot (born Giovanni Caboto) was, like Columbus, a native of Genoa who sought backing from a European power to venture overseas. In 1497, five years after Columbus's first landing in the Caribbean, Cabot attempted a similar journey, also in the belief that he would reach the mainland of Asia via a westerly course.

Fifty-two days after setting sail from Bristol with one ship and a small crew, Cabot landed on a barren, darkly forested shore. Cabot and his men erected a cross and an English banner before continuing to sail along the coast. He named the dark forests Newfoundland.

"To conquer, occupy, and possess."

—HENRY VII OF ENGLAND

A dispatch written c. 1498, after Cabot returned to England, indicates that, according to expedition members, the new land was inhabited by a "strange race of beings":

They found a trail that went inland, they saw a site where a fire had been made, they saw manure of animals that they thought to be farm animals. All along the coast they found many fish like those in Iceland which are dried in the open and sold in England and other countries. And thus following the shore, they saw two forms running on land one after the other, but they could not tell if they were human beings or animals.

Predictions and Prophecies

As with other tribes around the hemisphere, the spiritual elders of the North had been predicting the coming of the white man for some time before his actual arrival.

Not long before the Ojibwa of Canada saw their first European, one of their prophets had a painful and vivid dream:

"Men of strange appearance have come across the great water. They have landed on our island [North America]. Their skins are white like snow, and on their faces long hair grows. These people have come across the great water in wonderfully large canoes which have great white wings like those of a giant bird. The men have long and sharp knives, and they have long black tubes which they point at birds and animals. The tubes make a smoke that rises into the air just like the smoke from our pipes. From them come fire and such terrific noise that I was frightened even in my dreams."

Above: *An Ojibwa drum with traditional decoration from the Great Lakes region.*

Columbus had returned to Spain with less than he had hoped or promised to show for his voyages, but with stories that fired the imagination of those who heard them. Other Spanish explorers were inspired to continue the conquest of the Americas. By 1511, they were already well established in Cuba and on other islands.

Juan Ponce de León, governor of the Spanish colony on Puerto Rico, had been with Columbus on his second voyage, in 1493. In 1513 he sailed northwestward in search of a land that he had heard contained not only gold, but magical rejuvenating waters—the Fountain of Youth.

Just before Easter (*Pascua Florida*), Ponce de León and his crew made landfall on a peninsula that they believed to be an island. Because of the religious feast, or the profusion of flowers (*flores*), he christened his new discovery "*Florida*." He was not alone in appreciating the beauty of the land. Warriors of the Calusa, who inhabited the southern half of the peninsula, showered his party with arrows.

Right: A fortified village in Florida, by German engraver Theodor De Bry. The protective walls would not hold the Europeans, or their diseases, at bay for long.

Opposite: Two of Spain's most notorious sixteenth-century conquístadores: Vasco Núñez de Balboa (above), shown assuming an air of instant authority; and Pánfilo de Narváez arriving in Mexico in 1520, as seen by an Aztec artist.

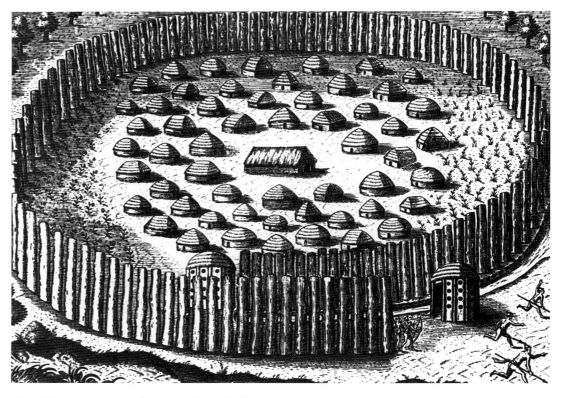

The Calusa were one of many tribes who lived in the Southeast and whose combined numbers have been estimated at one million. Having learned something of the Spanish via trading visits to Cuba, they were not interested in having anything to do with disease-bearing, slave-taking looters.

Ponce de León left, returning to Florida in 1521 with two hundred men, livestock, seeds, and priests. He had barely set foot on shore when a Calusa arrow bestowed a mortal wound. No record survives of the casualties his party inflicted on the Calusa.

The Cuba-based Spanish soon discovered the Yucatán peninsula, after a Spanish shipwreck there in 1511. Following an unsuccessful attempt by Francisco Hernández to invade the peninsula, a young administrator with ambitions to explore, Hernán Cortés, set out to find the rumored riches of what is now Mexico.

One of the great ironies of history is that 1519, the year of Cortés's voyage, was also the Aztec year "One Reed," in which the great god Quetzalcoatl had promised to return to his people to reclaim his rightful throne and kill all usurpers. Quetzalcoatl had been worshiped in the Central American region for centuries. According to ancient Toltec prophecy, "If he comes…on One Reed, he strikes at kings." Before Cortés arrived, a comet had been interpreted by Montezuma, leader of the Aztecs, as an augury of impending doom. For these reasons, Montezuma was terrified by the arrival of unknown white men from across the waters.

"I grieve to myself that ever this dwelling on earth should end. I foresaw, being a Mexican, that our rule began to be destroyed, I went forth weeping."

—FROM *Ancient Nahuatl Poetry*

The Conquistadors

The men who journeyed from Spain to explore the newly discovered Western hemisphere were ambitious for military and political advancement as well as personal fortunes. They had a blind loyalty to the Spanish monarchy and to the Roman Catholic Church that was closely identified with it. They were willing to take great risks and to expose others to many hardships in pursuit of their goals. And they could be quite as ruthless toward one another as they were toward the natives they plundered. When Pánfilo de Narváez was dispatched to Mexico in 1520 to replace the recalcitrant Hernán Cortés, he was promptly shut up in prison by his rival and kept there for several years. Backbiting, infighting, false reports, vanity, and deception marked the steady course of the conquistadors across the New World. Small wonder that their arrival inspired dismay among the native peoples.

Right: *A fanciful depiction of Juan Ponce de León, the Spanish explorer who named Florida, finding the mysterious Fountain of Youth, the magical spring he had learned about from Caribbean natives.*

Below: *A depiction of the arrival of Hernán Cortés in Mexico. The Aztecs believed that Cortés was a vengeful god whose appearance that year had long been prophesied.*

When they first beheld these white men, strange in appearance and with unfamiliar ways, Montezuma's messengers recorded their impressions, which have survived in Book 12 of the Florentine Codex, a history of the conquest written by Aztecs in the 1550s:

> A thing like a stone ball comes out of [the cannon's] entrails, raining fire and shooting sparks. And the smoke that comes out of it has a foul smell, like rotten mud, which assaults the brain....Their weapons and equipment are all made of iron. They dress in iron; they wear iron helmets on their heads; their swords are iron; their bows are iron; their shields are iron; their spears are iron....
>
> Their bodies are covered everywhere; only their faces can be seen. They are very white, as if made of lime....Their dogs are huge, with flat waving ears and long, gangling tongues.

The chroniclers continued: "When Motecuhzoma [Montezuma] heard this news, he was filled with terror. It was as if his heart grew faint, as if it shrank; he was overcome by despair." One of Cortés's men, soldier and chronicler Bernal Díaz, also found the encounter with a new culture awe-inspiring. He declared the Aztec land a marvel, reporting:

When we saw all those cities and villages built in the water, and other great towns on dry land, and that straight and level causeway leading to Mexico, we were astounded. These majestic towers and pyramids and houses rising from the water, all made of massive stone, seemed like an enchanted vision. Indeed, some of our men even asked if what we saw was not a dream.

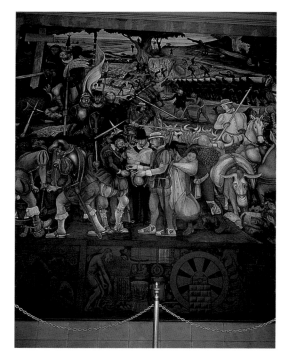

It was these beautiful cities and the highly developed culture so admired by Díaz that Cortés and company would destroy. During his inland march toward the capital, Mexico City, Cortés encountered resistance at Cholula:

There arose from the Spaniards a cry summoning all the noblemen, lords, war leaders, warriors and common folk; and when they had crowded into the temple courtyard, then the Spaniards blocked the entrances and every exit. There followed a butchery of stabbing, beating, killing of the unsuspecting Cholulans.... They were treacherously, deceitfully slain.

By the time the Spanish party reached Mexico City, Montezuma knew of the Cholula massacre. "Shocked, terrified," according to the scribes of the Florentine Codex, "Montezuma wept in the distress he felt for the city." His worst fears were justified, and it was surely of no comfort when he found, on face-to-face contact, that the aggressor was not Quetzalcoatl but a mere mortal. Cortés overwhelmed Montezuma's defenses and arrested the ruler, threatening him until he agreed to comply with a list of demands.

"They were utterly possessed by greed."

—AZTEC SCRIBE

After Montezuma had been pressured into signing papers that would, under Spanish law, make him a subject of the king of Spain, the invaders appropriated his possessions, "like little beasts, patting each other on the back, and their hearts were filled with delight...they were transported to the brink of lunacy. They rushed in everywhere, each one grasping for himself. They were utterly possessed by greed," reports the Florentine Codex. The treasures included "a quetzal plume headdress, featherwork pectorals, fine shields, golden discs, necklaces of the gods, gold nose pieces, bracelets, and diadems all of gold." The loot-

Left: *Detail of a tapestry from c. AD 1100. The conquistadors systematically looted art treasures as they found them.*

Below: *The first sheet of the official land grant issued by Spain's King Charles V, authorizing Cortés to conquer the territory that would soon be known in Europe as New Spain.*

Sacrifice!

One Aztec practice the Catholic invaders found shocking was the ritual sacrifice of humans. A sixteenth-century chronicler, who pointed out that non-Aztec war captives were selected for sacrifice whenever possible, described the ritual in vivid detail:

The manner they used in these Sacrifices, was, they assembled within the Palissadoe of dead mens Sculles such as should be sacrificed, using a certayne Ceremony at the foot of the Palissadoe, placing a great guard about them. Presently there stept forth a Priest, attyred with a short Surplice full of tassels beneath, who came from the top of the Temple with an Idoll made of Paste of Wheate and Mays [corn] mingled with Honey, which had the eyes made of the graines of greene glasse, and the teeth of the graines of Mays. He descended the steps of the Temple with all the speed he could, and mounted on a great stone planted upon a high Terrasse in the midst of the Court. This stone was called Quauxicalli, which is to say, the stone of Eagle, whereon he mounted by a little Ladder, which was in the fore-part of the Terrasse, and descended by another staire on the other side, still imbracing his Idoll. Then did he mount to the place where those were that should be sacrificed, shewing this Idoll to every one in particular, saying unto them; this is your God. And having ended his shew, he descended by the other side of the staires, and all such as should dye, went in procession unto the place where they should bee sacrificed, where they found the Ministers ready for that Office. The ordinary manner of sacrificing was, to open the stomake of him that was sacrificed, and having pulled out his heart halfe alive, they tumbled the man downe the staires of the Temple, which were all imbrewed and defiled with bloud: And to make it the more plaine, six Sacrificers being appointed to this dignitie, came into the place of Sacrifice, foure to hold the hands and feet of him that should be sacrificed, the fift to hold his head, and the sixt to open his stomake, and to pull out the heart of the sacrificed.

—José de Acosta, *The Natural and Moral History of the Indies*, 1590
(English translation, 1625)

ers summarily melted down the gold for convenience of carrying and burned everything they saw no use for.

The cruel behavior of Cortés and his soldiers provoked increasing Aztec anger. In 1520, Montezuma was discovered killed—by the Spanish, according to the Aztec version of events—and left carelessly "tossed outside the royal houses" (as the Florentine Codex described). The Spanish however, denied responsibility for his murder, which was to prove the last straw for the Aztecs. The ensuing two months saw fierce fighting, which, with the simultaneous damage inflicted by a smallpox epidemic, resulted in devastation for the Aztecs. "There came a great sickness, a pestilence, the smallpox…spread over the people with great destruction of men. The brave Mexican warriors were weakened by it," the scribes lamented.

After the Aztec defeat, thousands of impoverished Spaniards and other Europeans descended on what was to be called New Spain, to zealously convert the natives to the Catholic faith—in most cases, to rape, loot, and pillage.

Opposite: Toltec ruins at Teotihuacan: the Street of the Dead and Pyramid of the Sun. Cortés's soldier and chronicler, Bernal Díaz, described the amazement of the Spanish invaders on their first sight of "a straight and level causeway" and "majestic towers and pyramids."

Left: Montezuma, emperor of the Aztecs (1502–20), was taken prisoner by the Spanish when he received Cortés at his court in Tenochtitlán, the island capital, in 1519. He died mysteriously a year later.

Left: The meeting between Cortés and Montezuma. The ensuing battles, combined with a devastating smallpox epidemic, marked the beginning of the end of the great Aztec Empire.

Right: *Francisco Pizarro's entry into Cuzco, the Inca capital, in 1533. Pizarro and his troops had already spent six destructive years marauding through Inca territory before they reached Cuzco.*

Francisco Pizarro Invades Inca Territory

One of the stories of gold and treasure that had begun to circulate among the Spanish concerned a land of enormous wealth to the south, in what is now Peru. In 1526, Francisco Pizarro, another ambitious explorer, encountered an Inca trading raft off the Central American Coast during a Pacific voyage. Finding gold on board the raft, Pizarro determined to locate the source of this bounty. With the aid of the raft's captured crew as guides, he entered Tumbes, the northernmost coastal city of the Inca empire, in 1527. Quoting from the *Requirimiento*, a Papal order that legitimized (to Spanish eyes) foreign conquest in order to bring new people into the Catholic faith, he announced to the local official:

I, Francisco Pizarro,…hereby notify and inform you that God placed one Saint Peter in charge over all peoples. And so I require you to recognize the Church as your Mistress. And if you do not do this…with the help of God I shall come mightily against you, and shall subject you to the yoke of the Church, and shall seize your women and children, and I shall make them slaves, to sell and dispose of as His Majesty commands, and I shall do all the evil and damage to you that I am able.

The proclamation may well have lost something in the translation rendered to the official.

To a greater extent than the Aztecs and the Maya, the Inca measured their wealth much as did the tribes of North America—not just in

---

"They were all encased [by armor] and their faces completely covered in wool, so that all that could be seen were their eyes."

—WAMAN PUMA

---

terms of gold, but in terms of their people. Inca rulers took good care of their subjects, providing generously for the weaker members of their society. Pizarro had found a civilization with cities, roads, a detailed population census, and advanced agricultural techniques, as well as the precious metals he sought. Three years after this first visit, Pizarro returned with the official sanction of the Spanish Crown to invade Peru.

> *"We do not read in all the histories of Asia, Africa, or Europe that ever those kings were so gracious to their subjects as these."*
>
> —GARCILASO DE LA VEGA

In 1532, he traveled to the town of Cajamarca for his first meeting with the recently established Inca ruler, Atawallpa, who offered him a welcoming drink. "The Spaniard took it from his hand and tipped it on the ground, which angered my uncle very much," recalled Titu Kusi Yupanki in his 1570 record of the encounter. Pizarro then delivered the *Requirimiento* to the uncomprehending and offended ruler, and the hostile meeting was over. Pizarro's men attacked the city, killing thousands, and "when they were all dead, they took my uncle Atawallpa to a cell, where they kept him…with a chain around his neck," according to Titu Kusi Yupanki.

Atawallpa offered Pizarro a room of gold and two rooms of silver in exchange for his freedom. The Spaniards took the treasure as quickly as it could be assembled, condemned Atawallpa of treason, and proceeded to kill him.

Pedro Cieza de León, the Spanish explorer who recorded detailed accounts of this period, commented that "It is no small sorrow to reflect that those Incas, even though they were heathens and idolaters, knew how to keep such good order…and that we Christians have destroyed so many kingdoms."

Garcilaso de la Vega's writing reflects similar sentiments. Born in 1539 of a royal Incan mother—a cousin of Atawallpa—and a Spanish father, Garcilaso moved to Spain (where he was called "El Inca") in 1559 and became a highly educated young man. He would later refute official Spanish accounts of how his mother's people lived and how their empire was destroyed. His *Royal Commentaries* were first published in 1609, to great acclaim. He described the high culture of one of the Incan cities, Tawantinsuyu, as the ideal state: "The Incas were not only contented to bestow on their subjects their food and raiment, but many other presents. We do not read in all the histories of Asia, Africa, or Europe that ever those kings were so gracious to their subjects as these."

Perhaps more compelling reading, to some of his contemporaries, was Garcilaso's description of the Inca treasures at the temple of Cuzco:

> This Garden was in the Incas time a Garden of Silver and Gold, as they had in the Kings houses, where they had many sorts of Hearbes, Flowers, Plants, Trees, Beasts great and small, wilde,

Above: *A gold pendant of Inca workmanship. The precious metal was a primary incentive for the conquistadors; often, they melted down gold artifacts to make portable ingots.*

Left: *Gold earplugs made in Peru during the fourth or fifth century* AD. *The elaborate engraving demonstrates the sophistication of Inca craftsmanship.*

tame, Snakes, Lizards, Snailes, Butterflies, small and great Birds, each set in their place. They had Maiz, Quinva, Pulse, Fruit-trees with the fruite on them all of Gold and Silver. Like to this Temple of Cozco were others in many Provinces of that Kingdome, in which every Curaca indevoured according to his power to have such riches of Gold and Silver.

The Spanish Explore North America

In 1539, underwritten by the gold of Atawallpa, Hernando de Soto, Pizarro's lieutenant, landed in Florida, where he hoped to find a land of plenty for himself. Today, Americans are taught that de Soto was the "discoverer" of the Mississippi, along which he died in 1542 after conducting a brutal rampage through the Southeast. The determined conqueror brought with him a force of approximately six hundred soldiers and an undocumented number of slaves (some of them Incas), as well as horses and pigs.

In their attempts to deal with the invaders, native leaders relied upon an age-old method. Treating de Soto with polite caution, they assured him that the real gold was to be found over the next hill, beyond the next valley. On the party went, until disease and exhaustion finished most of them off (including, eventually, their leader). Garcilaso de la Vega recorded in his history *The Florida of the Inca* the reaction of Acuera, Timicua chief, to the invaders in 1539:

To me you are professional vagabonds who wander from place to place, gaining your livelihood by robbing, sacking and murdering people who have given you no offense. I want no manner of friendship or peace with people such as you, but instead prefer mortal and perpetual enmity.

Heading north, through the fertile country of present-day Georgia and into the Carolinas, de Soto followed a trail he hoped would lead

> ## "I and all of my people have vowed to die a hundred deaths to maintain the freedom of our land."
>
> ### —ACUERA, TIMICUA CHIEF, 1549

Right: *An early European depiction of the future Port Royal, Florida; Spanish, French, and British forces would fight for the region until 1821.*

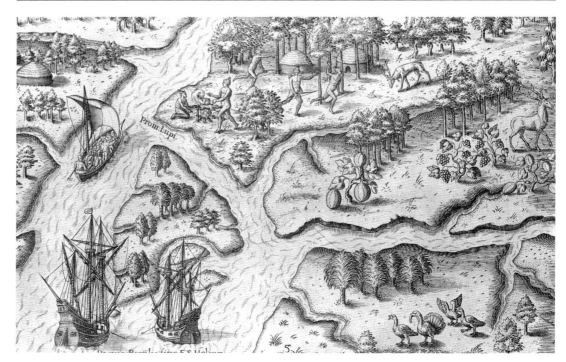

him to the wealthy state of Cofitachequi, of which he had heard promising rumors. In early 1540, he entered the state's capital city, Talomeco, and met the young woman who ruled there—a woman compared enthusiastically by one of de Soto's men to the formidable and beautiful Cleopatra. The city proved, indeed, to be rich, and its culture made an immediate impression on the newcomers—despite the fact that European disease (probably smallpox) had already caused havoc in the area, presumably having spread inland from an earlier Spanish landing. Garcilaso reported that the Spaniards had "found the town of Talomeco without any people at all, because the recent pestilence had raged with more virulence and cruelty in this town than in any other of the entire province. It is said they found four longhouses filled with bodies from the plague."

Even if the aftermath of disease was as Garcilaso described it, eyewitness Rodrigo Ranjel, de Soto's secretary, was sufficiently impressed by what he saw to write:

The people [of Cofitachequi] are very clean and polite. The chief Indians came with gifts [and the ruler was carried] in a litter covered with delicate white linen. She was a young girl of fine bearing; and she took off a string of pearls and put it on the Governor as a necklace to show her favor.

De Soto responded to the ruler's hospitable gesture by stripping down the temples and stores of the city of Talomeco and seizing everything in sight: pearls, weapons, food—and the ruler herself, leaving only the plague in his wake. Later, the ruler escaped, perhaps returning to the ruined city; her fate is unknown. De Soto and his party headed on, in search of the next windfall.

Later the same year, they reached Cherokee territory. Word of the invaders had traveled, apparently, and Rodrigo Ranjel recorded one encounter with a chief who, perhaps out of fear generated by the rumors, "gave the Christians whatever they asked—bearers, corn, dogs, and as much as he had." By October,

Above: *Hernando de Soto, a sixteenth-century Spanish explorer, invaded Florida in search of personal fame and wealth, namely gold. To this end, the means could be ruthless, as in this unprovoked attack.*

Above: *De Soto discovers the Mississippi River in this romanticized depiction of the explorer's erratic progress through the Southeast.*

however, they met a less compliant Choctaw chief, Tuscaloosa, who delayed the party before leading them into a trap, a well-planned attack in which many of the surviving Spanish party, and their animals, were killed.

De Soto was to continue his looting and burning through the Southeast for another two years before contracting a disease that would prove fatal.

While de Soto was in the Southeast, Spanish explorers were also at work on the western side of the continent. Coming up from Mexico City (where exotic goods from "El Norte" were traded), Francisco Vasquez de Coronado conquered Hawikuh, a Zuñi pueblo in what is now New Mexico, in July 1540. He was drawn in this direction by the good news of one Fray Marcos de Niza, who had viewed the pueblo from a hazy distance and reported that it was "bigger than the city of Mexico." Tales abounded that Hawikuh was but the smallest of seven cities under one lord, in a region called Cibola, where "women wore strings of gold beads and men girdles of gold." Whether they were trying to be helpful or merely to help the Spaniard quickly on his way is not known.

Coronado went from Hawikuh to Tiwa country, where he committed atrocities that caused many natives to flee into the mountains. When no gold was found, he moved on again, now in search of the riches of another fabled land, Gran Quivira.

"Think, then, what must be the effect of the sight of you and your people…astride the fierce brutes, your horses, entering with such speed and fury into my country. [It is] to strike awe and terror into our hearts."

—Chief of the Ichisi, 1540

His expedition traveled six hundred miles through present-day New Mexico, Texas, and Kansas. Great expanses of grass and thousands of buffalo were found, but no great cities arose from the plains, nor did precious metals present themselves. After a two-year foray, Coronado returned to Mexico, where his venture—having lost two-thirds of its men and found no gold—was regarded as a failure. Twelve years later, he died in obscurity and poverty. Three of the Franciscan friars who had remained behind to convert Hawikuh discovered "treasure" in the form of souls to save. Franciscan missionaries would become a powerful presence in the Southwest. Hernando de Alarcon, meanwhile, was leading yet another Spanish party through California.

"Seven Cities And Not An Ounce Of Gold."

—Francisco Coronado

Above: As the Spanish continued to use Mexico as a base for exploration and conquest farther north, the Aztecs used human sacrifice to appease their angry gods. Here, Aztec priests offer human hearts to Huitzilopochtli, the god they believed to be the "omen of evil [and] creator of war."

Left: Francisco Coronado sets out on his futile two-year, 600-mile search for the mythical Gran Quivira.

Above: Gold for the taking! A sixteenth-century engraving shows native laborers extracting the precious metal from a riverbed for the Spanish.

A Stirring of Spanish Conscience

Eventually, it was inevitable that the methods of the Spanish explorers would attract opposition within Spain. A Dominican missionary who had accompanied conquistadors in South and Central America for three decades, Bartolomé de Las Casas, was fiercely critical of the conquerors of Mexico and the Caribbean islands. Horrified at their cruelty, he recounted his time in Cuba (1513–20) in his *Brief Report on the Destruction of the Indians*:

> One time the Indians came to meete us, and to receive us with victuals, and delicate cheere, and with all entertainment ten leagues off a great Citie, and being come at the palace, they presented us with a great quantity of fish, and of bread, and other meate, together with all that they could doe for us to the uttermost. See incontinent the

Divell [Devil], which put himselfe into the Spaniards, to put them all to the edge of the sword in my presence, without any cause whatsoever, more than three thousand soules, which were set before us, men, women, and children. I saw there so great crueltics, that never any man living either have or shall see the like….

After that the Indians of this Island [Cuba] were thus brought into bondage and calamitie, like unto those of the Ile of Hispaniola, and that they saw that they died and perished all without remedy: some of them began to flye into the Mountaines, others quite desperate hanged themselves, and there hung together husbands with their wives, hanging with them their little children. And through the crueltie of one only Spaniard, which was a great tyrant, and one whom I know, there hung themselves more *than two hundred Indians: and in this fashion died an infinitie of people....In three or foure moneths (my selfe being present) there died more then sixe thousand children, by reason that they had plucked away from them their fathers and mothers, which they sent into the Mines.*

His accounts of brutalities so embarrassed the Spanish Crown that it called for a debate whose purpose was to determine whether or not the natives were to be considered human. The debate was held before the Council of the Indies in Valladolid in 1550. Las Casas defended the natives, while his main opponent, Dr. Juan Ginés de Sepulveda, declared:

You will scarcely find traces of humanity [in the natives] who...are so cowardly and timid, that they scarcely withstand the appearance of our soldiers, fleeing like women before a very few Spaniards.

His argument rested on the fashionable Aristotelian doctrine of natural slavery, which held that the superior ruled for the benefit of the inferior (slaves), who otherwise were incapable of governing themselves. No mention was made of the effective government they already had.

After years of argument, Las Casas's side finally won the day, at least on paper. The Papal Bull of 1537, *Sublimus Deus*, reversed that of 1493, part of the *Requirimiento* that Pizarro had read to the Inca:

We consider, however, that the Indians are truly men....the said Indians are by no means to be deprived of their liberty or the possession of their property; and that they may and should, freely and legitimately, enjoy their liberty and possession of their property; nor should they be in any way enslaved; should the contrary happen, it shall be null and of no effect.

Below: *The Spanish "crueltie" described by Las Casas drove many natives to suicide to avoid an even more brutal fate.*

The Visitors Settle In

"You say: Why do not the Indians till the ground and live as we do? May we not ask, why the white people do not hunt and live as we do?"

—Corn Tassel, Cherokee, 1785

During most of the sixteenth century, Spanish conquistadors focused their attention on shipping the wealth of Mexico to Spain. Those few who adventured into the present-day South and Southwest left few traces of themselves beyond a few coins and helmets. However, they did introduce European diseases, which began to reduce native North American populations.

In the late sixteenth century, the Spanish of New Spain began to establish missions in the Pueblo country of what is now New Mexico, creating outposts of their growing empire. Concerned about English exploration along the Pacific coast, they claimed what is now California.

As the Europeans continued to wage war upon each other at home, they looked abroad to replenish their finances. The English and the Dutch had been exposed to New World wealth while supplying the Spanish with African slaves; they began to establish their own North American bastions, closely followed by the French and others.

During the sixteenth and seventeenth centuries, the Europeans made inroads into North America from several directions: the Spanish from the south and west, the British and French from the north and east. The Dutch established New Netherland along the Hudson River. With an arrogance born partly of their inability to see native peoples as human, Europeans divided the entire continent among themselves, planting flags and proclaiming ownership wherever they set foot.

Even if North America had proven to contain little or no gold, fertile lands and forests full of game would have been sufficiently attractive. The European powers made individual trading partnerships with the tribes they met. They provided the Indians with guns, rum, and metalware, in return for beaver pelts and other animal skins that were scarcer in Europe, where many forests had been cut down. Especially in the colder climates of what is now Canada, where fur was thick and plentiful, the trade in pelts was extremely lucrative.

Opposite: *The "purchase" of Manhattan from the Lenape by Dutch colonists, 1626. The island changed hands for a collection of trinkets whose value was estimated at twenty-five dollars—treasures greatly exaggerated in this romanticized depiction.*

Left: *Jacques Cartier's navigation up the St. Lawrence River in 1535 secured France's claim to Canada. Cartier had set out to find the coveted Northwest Passage to the Orient.*

Right: Before contact, an estimated 500 native nations inhabited North America; their lifeways varied widely according to climate and terrain. The arctic tribes were the least affected by colonial settlers (although they did not escape the impact of colonial-era diseases brought by explorers). The traditional igloo still provides shelter for a small minority of arctic peoples today.

In the early 1600s, there were at least five hundred distinct tribal groups of native people all across Turtle Island—the name some tribes had given to their continental homeland. The European wars would be extended into North America as the major powers vied with each other for native allies and trading partners. From the beginning, relations were marked by ambivalence. While native people were drawn to the unfamiliar goods brought by the whites, few were impressed by European values or by the Europeans themselves. In fact, they were widely regarded as unscrupulous, unclean, and devoid of spirituality.

Like the native nations, the Europeans differed from each other in language, religion, and culture. But they had more in common with each other than with their native neighbors. Their attitude toward the indigenous peoples was primarily condescending, where it was not downright ruthless. They were convinced that their culture and religion were superior. Some were sincerely concerned with evangelizing the native peoples, whom they saw as pagans in danger of "losing their souls." But the majority wanted wealth and/or land and felt a strong sense of entitlement to them. Throughout the next two centuries, native peoples would be pushed off their traditional holdings and crowded into smaller and smaller enclaves. Trading partnerships between the various tribes and European powers, and the changing alliances and conflicts among them all, mark the history of these two centuries. Many powerful native groups, including the Iroquois Confederacy of New York, would play decisive roles.

Land of Many Nations

When Europeans began their invasion of North America in the late fifteenth century, the total native population has been variously estimated at between 2 and 10 million. The people spoke hundreds of different languages and had widely divergent ways of life, rituals, and beliefs. They traded not only with neighboring groups but with those at great distances. Alliances were formed and re-formed on the basis of mutual needs and antipathies.

While specific beliefs differed from tribe to tribe, some values and attitudes were almost universal, from the seafaring peoples of the Northwest to the Cherokee nations of the Southeast. One unifying theme relates tribal heritage to the land itself.

> *"We stand somewhere between the mountain and the ant."*
>
> — ONONDAGA PROVERB

Indians lived in many different ways. Some were settled as farmers, like the Hopi; others fished and gathered shellfish, like the coastal peoples of both East and West; others, including the Plains and Plateau tribes, were hunters and gatherers. But without exception, they honored the earth that generated life, and considered all living things worthy of respect.

The Hopi attribute their principal food to the Corn Mothers—Blue Corn Woman and White Corn Maiden—who brought it with them when they climbed through the kiva roof onto Earth's surface. At birth, every child is given a symbolic ear of corn. Within the month, as described in an ancient ceremonial, he or she is entrusted to a higher power:

When a child was born, his Corn Mother was placed beside him for twenty days, during which he was kept in darkness. Early on the morning of the twentieth day, the mother took the child in her arms and the Corn Mother in her right hand. Accompanied by her own mother—the child's grandmother—she left the house and walked toward the east. When they stopped, facing east, they prayed silently and cast pinches of cornmeal toward the rising sun. When the sun cleared the horizon, the mother stepped forward, held up the child, and said, "Father Sun, this is your child."

Native people celebrated the sacredness of all things. Spirituality was not something reserved for a special day or a special building. Sacredness was omnipresent, as expressed in the words of Oglala Sioux holy man Black Elk, who recounted in his 1947 autobiography, *Black Elk Speaks*, the words of a guardian spirit, White Buffalo Calf Woman: "All of this [world] is sacred, and so do not forget. Every dawn as it comes is a holy event, and every day is

Below: In more amenable climates, native American agricultural techniques were highly developed long before the arrival of the colonists, whose survival depended on acquiring their expertise. This engraving depicts the sowing of maize and beans in sixteenth-century Florida.

Right: Taos Pueblo, New Mexico: a dwelling in the multistory adobe complex today, virtually unchanged since long before the coming of the Spanish.

Opposite above: Two Pima women of present-day Arizona as seen by a colonist. The ancestors of the Pima and neighboring Papago tribes have inhabited this semiarid region continuously for an estimated 9,000 years.

Opposite below: Remains of a six-story structure, part of an indigenous settlement at Pueblo Bonito in western New Mexico, built around AD 919.

holy…and also you must always remember that the two-leggeds and all the other peoples who stand upon this earth are sacred and should be treated as such."

When white settlers and traders began arriving in the early 1600s, there were few broad alliances among the many tribes. Powhatan's great confederacy of fourteen thousand people in thirty-two tribes along the Chesapeake had few counterparts outside of Central America. Unlike the Iroquois Confederacy farther north, Powhatan's alliance was loosely formed, and he did not seek to extend it. He could have wiped out the English settlement at Jamestown, but chose not to do so.

The Iroquois Confederacy was the most powerful native alliance. It had been formed in the mid-1500s in response to constant warring among Northeastern tribes. When the Europeans arrived, the confederacy consisted of the Five Nations: Seneca, Cayuga, Onondaga, Oneida, and Mohawk. It was bounded by Lake Ontario to the north, and included parts of modern Pennsylvania, New York, Vermont, and Ontario. The Iroquois had developed a unified system of shell currency—wampum—that regulated trade and had organized for warfare against adversarial tribes. They would be the strongest political force at the inception of the great struggle for territory, with European powers vying for their support.

The Colonists of Western North America

At its height, the Spanish empire extended from the headwaters of the Rio Grande in the north to the Rio de la Plata in the south, from Florida in the east to California in the west. At first, the Spanish concentrated on the vast mineral wealth of Mexico and Peru. The apparently inhospitable lands of the North American Southwest, as well as disappointment in the early searches for gold, helped spare the Pueblo peoples from invasion. However, by 1598 Spanish interest turned to the Rio Grande Valley, where some fifty thousand Indians lived in sixty riverside communities.

In 1598, Don Juan de Oñate was granted all of present-day New Mexico to found a permanent colony at his own expense. He traveled to the upper Rio Grande Valley with eighty wagons, seven thousand head of livestock, several hundred families, and eight Franciscan friars. At the Tewa pueblo of San Juan, he prevailed upon the native priests to yield up part of the community to the Spanish colonists without bloodshed. The newcomers called their settlement San Gabriel and built a small church nearby. They undertook an aggressive missionary campaign among the pueblo peoples.

When the Sky City of Acoma attacked a force led by Oñate's nephew, killing him and ten other Spaniards, the pueblo was burned and some 800 inhabitants were massacred. Survivors were indentured for twenty years as slaves of the Spanish officials, colonists, and missionaries. As a warning to the other pueblos, the men were also sentenced to public mutilation.

For more than eighty years, the Spanish colonized the pueblos. Eventually, many Franciscan missions were built in New Mexico on orders from the new Spanish capital, called Santa Fe (Holy Faith). Despite the good motives of many of the Franciscan missionaries, the incursion undermined the culture of native society.

The pueblos quietly resisted the Franciscans' efforts. Using the same strategy that Inca ruler Manco Capac had urged on his people before his death, they converted openly to Christianity and continued to practice their religion secretly. When the anticipated gold and silver did not materialize in the deserts of New Mexico, Oñate and his successors worked the Indians oppressively to regain their financial investment, demanding both labor and tribute.

The Pueblo Revolts

Harsh treatment by a succession of Spanish governors and missionaries eventually led to the first organized revolt of the Pueblo people in 1680. The concerted attack caught the Spanish off guard. Half the colonists were killed outright, and missions were burned.

Spanish inquisitors interrogated native prisoners to find out who had planned the revolt. Pedro Naranjo of San Felipe, one of the prisoners, identified Popé, a San Juan medicine man, who claimed spiritual guidance for the rebellion. Popé had organized the alliance in which nineteen Rio Grande pueblos rose up to evict the Spanish. An inquisitor transcribed Naranjo's testimony, which alleged that Popé "commanded all the Indians to break the lands and enlarge their cultivated fields, saying that now they were as they had been in ancient times, free from the labor they had performed for the Spaniards, who could not now be alive." The transcription continues:

Right: *One of the many Franciscan missions that were built in New Mexico by the Spanish, who enforced their rule and religion on the Pueblo peoples.*

Asked why they so blindly burned the images, temples, crosses, and other things of divine worship, he [Pedro Naranjo] stated that the said Indian, Popé, came down in person, and with him El Saca and El Chato from the pueblo of Los Taos, and other captains and leaders and many people who were in his train, and he ordered in all the pueblos through which he passed that they instantly break up and burn the images of the holy Christ, the virgin Mary and the other saints, the crosses, and everything pertaining to Christianity, and that they burn the temples, break up the bells, and separate from the wives whom God had given them in marriage and take those whom they desired.

In order to take away their baptismal names, the water, and the holy oils, they were to plunge into the rivers and wash themselves with amole, which is a root native to the country, washing even their clothing, with the understanding that there would thus be taken from them the character of the holy sacraments. He [Popé] saw to it that they at once erected and rebuilt their houses of idolatry, which they call estufas, and made very ugly masks in imitation of the devil in order to dance the dance of the cacina [kachina]; and he said like-

wise that the devil had given them to understand that living thus in accordance with the law of their ancestors, they would harvest a great deal of maize, many beans, a great abundance of cotton, calabashes, and very large watermelons and cantaloupes; and that they could erect their houses and enjoy abundant health and leisure.

Thus the Spanish were barred from New Mexico for twelve years. However, the collapse of the Pueblo alliance reopened the door to occupation in 1692. The Spanish returned under Diego de Vargas, with a large force of Franciscan missionaries and over 1,000 colonists. In 1696, the pueblos rose again, but factionalism among their leaders prevented them from achieving their goal. However, the revolt of 1680 was a long-term success in that the Spanish never sought to impose their religion and culture with the same brutality. The Pueblo people, for their part, guarded their lifeways with greater vigilance, maintaining a high degree of cultural integrity that endures to this day. In the words of the Hopi: "Our land, our religion, and our life are one....It is upon this land that we have hunted deer, elk, antelope, buffalo, rabbit, turkey....It is from this land that we obtained the timbers and stone for our homes and kivas."

> ## "We will not sell our homes, our land, our religion, and our way of life for money."
>
> — HOPI ELDER

Some lessons were learned from the Pueblo revolts. Spanish friars who set out to evangelize California in 1769 were generally more tolerant of tribal practices. "Though all are Christians," one visitor would report of the mission Indians in 1827, "they still keep many of their old beliefs, which the padres, from policy, pretend not to know."

The initial purpose of the California missions was to preserve Spanish hegemony along the West Coast, where Russian traders had made inroads among the native peoples of the North-west. In what is now southern California, Spanish priests converted many of the native peoples and brought them to work in the missions.

At the age of thirteen, a Luiseño Indian named Pablo Tac described his experience at the Mission of San Luis Rey, near present-day Oceanside. In 1822, twenty-four years after the mission was founded, Tac became one of almost four thousand native children who had been baptized there:

The Father Peyri ordered the Indians to carry stone from the sea (which is not far) for the foundations, to make bricks, roof tiles, to cut beams, reeds, and what was necessary.... They made a church with three altars,... two chapels, two sacristies, two choirs, a flower garden for the church, a high tower with five bells, two small and three large, the cemetery with a crucifix in the middle for all who die here.

With the laborers goes a Spanish major-domo and others,...to hurry them if they

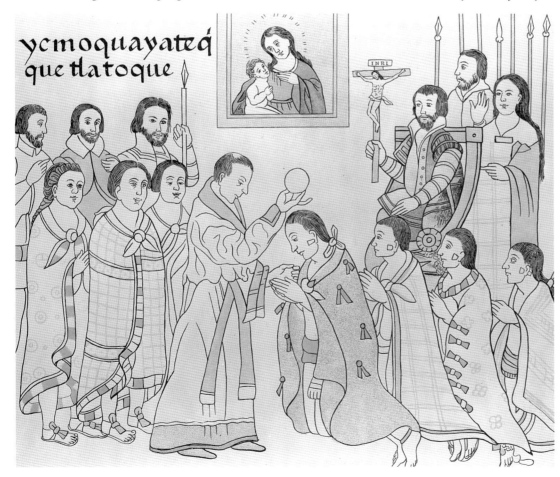

Left: In this sixteenth-century Mexican manuscript illustration, four of the converted receive the holy sacrament from a Catholic priest. The Spanish let it be known that only by adopting Christianity would the Pueblo peoples avoid further persecution. As Bernal Diaz put it, the purpose of the Spanish mission was "to serve God...to give light to those in darkness and also to get rich."

A Salish Legend of the Russians and Napoleon

This story from the early days of Northwestern coastal trade with Russia (from c. 1750) was transcribed by E. Pauline Johnson-Tekahionwake, a Mohawk writer, from an account by Squamish chief Capilano of Vancouver (c. 1906). The chief said that the tale had come "over the Pacific from the place they call Russia":

The only male member [of the tribe] living was a very old warrior, hero of many battles and possessor of a talisman that was proof against all evil. On his death-bed, his women of three generations gathered about him. But not one man, nor yet a boy of his own blood, stood by to speed his departing warrior spirit to the land of peace and plenty.

"The charm cannot rest in the hands of women," he murmured. "Women may not war and fight other nations or other tribes; women are for the peaceful lodge and for the leading of little children. The charm must go to one as unconquerable as I have been. When I am dead, send it across the great salt chuck to the victorious Frenchman; they call him Napoleon Bonaparte."

Next day, a small seal-hunting vessel anchored in the inlet. All the men aboard spoke Russian, except for two thin, dark sailors who kept aloof from the crew. These two came ashore and spoke in French with a wandering Hudson's Bay trapper, who often lodged with the Squamish people. Thus the women knew these two strangers to be from the land where the great Frenchman was fighting against the world.

"How came the Frenchmen in a Russian sealer?" asked the women of a bystander.

"Captives," was the reply. "Almost slaves, and hated by their captors as the majority always hate the few." Then the Squamish women spoke with the Frenchmen and persuaded them to take the talisman to Napoleon.

As the crew boarded the sealer, the women watching from the shore observed strange contortions seize many of the men: some fell on the deck, some crouched, shaking as with palsy; some writhed for a moment, then fell limp. Only the two Frenchmen stood erect and strong—the Squamish talisman had already overcome their foes. Eventually, the voices of the trumpets of war carried back to the wilds of the Pacific Coast the news that the great Squamish charm had reached Napoleon, and from that time onward his career was one vast victory.

Left: *The wampum belt, a form of currency among eastern North American tribes and used at the trading posts. Made of hard clamshells strung into patterns, wampum belts were also an indication of status in some tribes.*

Below: *French explorer Samuel de Champlain, shown symbolically claiming Quebec (1608). The fur-trade network that became established in the region helped solidify France's 125-year colonial empire.*

are lazy, so that they will soon finish what was ordered, and to punish the guilty or lazy one who leaves his plow and quits the field. They work all day, but not always. At noon they leave work, and then they bring them posole. They eat it with gusto, and they remain sated until afternoon, when they return to their villages. The shoemakers work making chairs, leather knapsacks, reins, and shoes for the cowboys and Spanish soldiers.

In the Mission of San Luis Rey de Francia, the Fernandino Father is like a king. He has his pages, alcaldes [officials], majordomos, musicians, soldiers, gardens, ranchos, livestock, horses by the thousand, cows, bulls by the thousand, oxen, mules, asses, twelve thousand lambs, two hundred goats....The products of the Mission are butter, tallow, hides, chamois leather, bear skins, wine, white wine, brandy, oil, maize, wheat, beans and also bull horns, which the English take by the thousand to Boston.

Between 1769, beginning with San Diego de Alcalá, and 1823, when the mission of San Francisco Solano was founded near what is today Sonoma, the Franciscans established a

Above: *Dutch houses in Albany, New York, as illustrated in the December 1789 issue of Columbian Magazine.*

Opposite: *"When I look upward, I see the sky serene and happy; and when I look on the earth, I see all my children wandering in the utmost misery and distress," lamented a Chippewa man during a devastating smallpox epidemic. Afflicted natives are shown succumbing to the deadly disease in this sixteenth-century drawing by Bernadino de Sahagun, a Spanish monk.*

series of twenty-one missions in California. Most of them became the sites of future cities, including Carmel, San Luis Obispo, San Francisco, Santa Clara, Santa Barbara, and Santa Cruz. However, Spain did not establish the strong hold on California that had been envisioned. Russian fur trading interests in Alaska continued to extend their outposts into northern California. In 1812, the Russians established Fort Ross on the northern coast. Limited in 1823 by the Monroe Doctrine, whereby the United States government declared that North and South America should be considered closed to European colonization, they agreed to confine their settlements to Alaska, where they had already wreaked havoc among the native Inuit and Northwest Coastal tribes. In fact, they did not leave the California region until the 1840s. By that time, California had become part of the Mexican Republic, formed after Mexico won independence from Spain in 1821.

Colonization in Eastern North America

Regular contact between Europeans and Northeastern native Americans is thought to have begun by the early 1500s, when Portuguese, Basque, and Breton fishermen visited the shores of Newfoundland. Although they did not settle there—the terrain and climate were inhospitable—there was an abundance of cod in the Newfoundland waters, and the Portuguese established a station for processing fish onshore. Their legacy was disease, making the Beothuk

among the first tribes to be diminished by European germs.

Dutch involvement in the New World began in 1609, when Henry Hudson, sailing for the Netherlands, discovered the river named for him. Five years later, a Dutch trading post—Fort Nassau—was built near what is now Albany, New York, and a trade agreement was made with the Mahican. When Fort Nassau was flooded, the Dutch West India Company built Fort Orange on the same site (1624).

Shortly thereafter, the Mohawks joined the Mahicans in trading with the Dutch. However, as growing numbers of Dutch settlers left their land-poor nation to become farmers in the rich river valleys of New Netherland, clashes became more frequent and destructive. The principal Dutch-colonial settlement was New Amsterdam, established in 1629 on the island of Manhattan. It would be renamed New York by the English, who took it over in 1664.

The worst example of Dutch treatment of the natives occured at Pavonia (now Jersey City, New Jersey) in 1634. Wappinger Indians pursued by the Mohawks sought refuge in Pavonia and nearby New Amsterdam, but the Dutch governor refused to shelter them and incited his Mohawk allies against them. The Mohawks killed some seventy Wappinger tribesmen. Then the governor, as reported by David Pieterszoon de Vries, a Dutch artilleryman, turned on the Wappinger survivors, most of them women and children. According to de Vries:

About midnight, I heard a great shrieking, and I ran to the ramparts of the fort, and looked over to Pavonia. Saw nothing but firing, and heard the shrieks of the Indians murdered in their sleep....When it was day the soldiers returned to the fort, having massacred or murdered eighty Indians, and considering that they had done a deed of Roman valour in murdering so many in their sleep; where infants were torn from their mother's breasts, and hacked to pieces in the presence of the parents, and the pieces thrown into the fire and in the water, and other sucklings being bound to small boards, and then cut, stuck, and pierced, and miserably massacred in a manner to move a heart of stone. Some were thrown into the river, and when the fathers and mothers endeavoured to save them, the soldiers would not let them come on land, but made both parents and children drown—children from five to six years of age, and also some old and decrepit persons....As soon as the Indians understood that the [Dutch] had so treated them, all the men whom they could surprise on the farm-lands, they killed; but we never heard that they have ever permitted women or children to be killed.

Dutch hegemony in the colonies along the Delaware and Hudson Rivers was short-lived, but the alliance the Dutch formed with the Mohawks and other Iroquois—called the Covenant Chain—had far-reaching results. When the English took over the Dutch colony, they turned the Convenant Chain into an English-Iroquois alliance against the French.

Jacques Cartier, who established a French colony in Quebec in 1534, and the French explorers who followed him in the sixteenth century advised France of the vast supplies of fish and fur to be found in North America. They laid claim to the territory that included the St. Lawrence River Valley, the Great Lakes, and the Mississippi River Valley. The land they occupied was home to the Algonquian tribes of the Great Lakes (including the Mahicans, Ottowa, and Ojibwa), the Maritimes (including the Abenaki, Penobscot, and Micmac), the Subarctic (Cree and Montagnais); and the Iroquois, including the Mohawk and Huron tribes. Eventually, French explorers and traders

Alcohol and Disease: Destructive Imports

As with those who met the Spanish conquistadors to the south, the North American tribes were decimated by European diseases, including smallpox, measles, and other infections. Their lack of resistance to these virulent new contagions took a heavy toll of the population. And the alcohol introduced by European traders was just as deadly in its own ways. Most tribes were unaccustomed to it and did not know how to drink in moderation. Drunkenness eroded family and tribal ties, and good judgment. It was fostered by unscrupulous traders to gain the advantage in negotiations. In the mid-seventeenth century, Catawba chieftain Haglar complained to North Carolina authorities about the use of alcohol against his people. King Haglar, as the English called him, petitioned repeatedly for an embargo on hard liquor: "You sell it to our young men and give it [to] them many times; they get very drunk with it [and] this is the very cause that they ofttimes commit those crimes that is offensive to you and us, and all through the effect of that drink. It is also very bad for our people, for it rots their guts and causes our men to get very sick, and many of our people [have] lately died by the effects....I heartily wish you would do something to prevent your people from daring to sell or give them any of that strong drink." Unfortunately, this remonstration and others like it were largely ignored, and alcoholism became an increasingly serious problem in native communities. In the early 1700s, a Mahican delegation complained to the governor of New York that "When our people come from hunting to the town or plantations and want powder, and shot, and clothing, they first give us a large cup of rum. After we get the taste for it we crave for more so that in the end all the beaver and peltry we have hunted goes for drink, and we are left destitute."

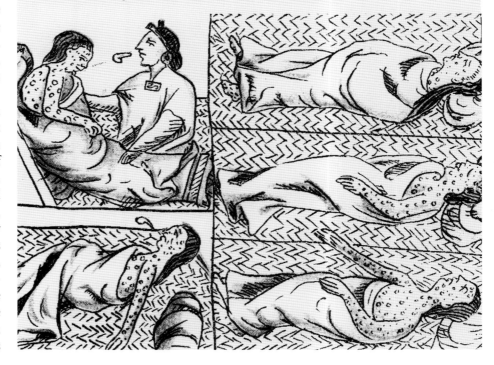

were followed by colonists to what was called New France. Most of the larger French settlements, like Quebec and Montreal, were established in Canada, but smaller communities grew up around their thriving trading posts, especially along the Mississippi River.

The Fur Trade

Soon after the arrival of the first French settlers in the late fifteenth century, regular trade began to develop between the newcomers and native trappers, who exchanged beaver, otter, and fox pelts for tools, cloth, utensils, and European foods. While the men of the Great Lakes and Subarctic tribes were experienced trappers, the women had sophisticated skills in cleaning, curing, and tanning pelts and hides for a variety of uses.

In 1608, Samuel de Champlain, who had been exploring and mapping the Atlantic coast for five years, received a royal charter for a permanent post on the Saint Lawrence River, and founded Quebec. The rivalry for the fur trade enabled Champlain to make alliances with Algonquian groups against the Iroquois Confederacy to the south.

Through the new Hudson's Bay Company, founded in 1670, the British soon joined the French in seeking furs, although they were less successful initially. While the French *voyageurs* and *couriers de bois* traveled into the wilderness, learned native languages, and fostered closer relationships with the trappers, the British generally stayed at their forts on the Hudson Bay, the biggest of which was York Fort. They did not expand into the interior to build their large network of trading posts until the eighteenth century.

"The beaver does everything perfectly well. It makes kettles, hatchets, swords, knives, bread. In short, it makes everything."

— MONTAGNAIS TRADER

The fur trade had several adverse effects upon the native peoples. First, the Europeans brought many diseases, which moved quickly through the encampments. By the early 1600s, smaller

Below: Peter Rindisbacher, an explorer who spent a winter at a Naskapi camp in Canada, said, "An Indian without snowshoes…is as helpless as a steamship without its engine," a point illustrated in his 1825 depiction of buffalo hunters.

tribes were becoming increasingly dependent upon European goods obtained by trapping beaver. One Montagnais trader joked that "The beaver does everything perfectly well. It makes kettles, hatchets, swords, knives, bread. In short, it makes everything." Alcohol was introduced, to harmful effect. Trapping began to take precedence over traditional hunting for food, and the eastern tribes soon trapped out their areas. They moved into neighboring territory, creating intertribal tension. One result was the Iroquoian Beaver Wars of 1638–84, which pitted the Iroquois Confederacy against tribes including the Hurons, Ottawas, and Mahicans.

The "Black Robes"

French missionaries of the Society of Jesus (Jesuits) had a more respectful attitude toward the native peoples than most Europeans. The "Black Robes," as they were called, learned native languages and went to live among the tribes to spread Christianity. Their conversions were slow but often proved lasting. They came to be trusted as men who kept their word and did not prey upon women or seek to enrich themselves. Early records of contact show mutual efforts to establish relationships, like the greeting extended to a Jesuit missionary by an Algonquian elder in northeastern Canada in 1670:

This is well, Black Gown, that thou comest to visit us. Take pity on us; thou art a Manitou [spirit]; we give thee tobacco to smoke. Let the earth give us corn, and the rivers yield us fish; let not disease kill us any more, or famine treat us any longer so harshly.

Above: *Weighing furs at a trading post, where disease and dependency were transferred along with the European goods exchanged for precious animal pelts.*

Left: *Rock Fort on the Hayes River in Canada was built in 1794 by the Hudson's Bay Company and was used during the fur trade as a warehouse for the smaller inland posts. Increasing competition between England and French Canada resulted in the construction of fortified posts.*

Above: *Fort Yukon, 1847, a Hudson's Bay Company holding on the Yukon River.*

Right: *An early engraving of the first French settlement at Quebec.*

leave their homes and kin for such extended periods. Hospitable offers of sharing traditional foods were frequently refused by the visitors, causing offense. The Jesuits, in turn, misread and often underestimated their hosts. One missionary to Quebec City complained:

The Indians prevent their [childrens'] instruction: they will not tolerate the chastisement of their children, whatever they may do…[and] they think they are doing you some great favor in giving you their children to instruct, to feed, and to dress. Besides, they will ask a great many things in return, and will be very importunate in threatening to withdraw their children, if you do not accede to their demands.

A Huron elder complained that "One does not see anything else but little Indians in the houses of the French….You are continually asking us for our children, and you do not give yours; I do not know any family among us which keeps a Frenchman with it."

The missionaries set out to convert their hosts on their own ground. Their vows of

However, the great disparity of culture fostered many misunderstandings. Although tribal elders usually isolated themselves for spiritual retreats, the Jesuit vow of lifelong celibacy was regarded by most natives as unnatural, as was the obvious willingness of the missionaries to

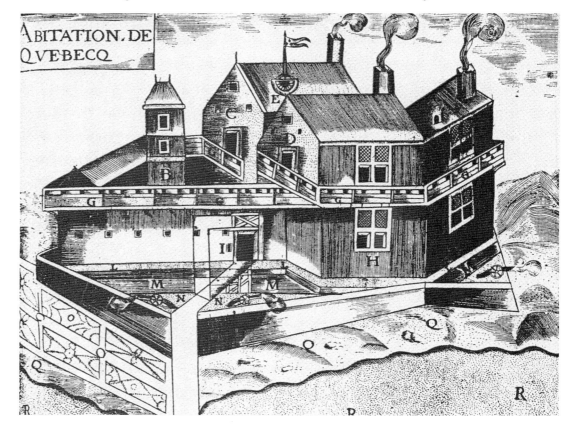

chastity and obedience to Church authorities were tested as they struggled to adapt to the extremes of climate as well as the cultural variances. In 1632, Father Paul Le Jeune recorded these impressions of his apparently primitive Montagnais neighbors:

Their only thought is to live. These people do not think there is any other science in the world except that of eating and drinking; and in this lies all their philosophy. They are astonished at the value we place upon books, seeing that a knowledge of them does not give us anything with which to drive away hunger. They cannot understand what we ask from God in our prayers. "Ask Him," they say to me, "for moose, bears, and beavers; tell him that thou wishest them to eat"; and when I tell them that those are only trifling things, that there are still greater riches to demand, they laughingly reply, "What couldst thou wish better than to eat thy fill of these good dishes?" In short, they have nothing but life; yet they are not always sure of that, since they often die of hunger.

Le Jeune soon learned, though, that the Montagnais had their own deeply held beliefs. On one occasion, he gave a piece of meat to the dogs, and was surprised when his hosts "commenced to cry out against me, saying that I was contaminating their feast,…and we should die of hunger." He had not shown proper respect to the animals that had been killed to be eaten. This breach of custom led to his local nickname "captain of the dogs." Le Jeune also remarked upon their social structure: "They have reproached me a hundred times because we fear our captains…. All the authority of their chief is in his tongue's end, for he is powerful in so far as he is eloquent; and, even if he kills himself talking and haranguing, he will not be obeyed unless he pleases [them]."

Both the culture clash and the new diseases contributed to a deterioration in relations, until the natives developed a profound mistrust of the missionaries' message, as evidenced in the words of an Algonquian elder, c. 1611: "I have been among the French at Quebec and at three Rivers; they taught me the foundation of their

Above: *A Cree family with traditional birchbark canoe and hide-covered tipi, camped alongside the La Grande River near Fort George, Quebec.*

Right: *This conical Montagnais tipi was a typical dwelling of the nomadic tribes, because it was easily constructed and dismantled.*

Montagnais Lodge at Mingan. July 23rd.

doctrine. But the more thoroughly I examined their mysteries, the less clearly I saw the light. They are tales invented to inspire us with true beliefs of an imaginary fire and under the false hope of a good which never will come to us." This sentiment was echoed more strongly in a 1642 Algonquian Council record:

It is a strange thing that since prayer has come into our cabins, our former customs are no longer of any service; and yet we shall all die because we give them up....I have seen the time when my dreams were true; when I had seen moose or beavers in sleep, I would take some [in the hunt]. When [our elders] felt the enemy coming, that came true; there was preparation to receive them. Now, our dreams and our prophecies are no longer true—prayer has spoiled everything for us.

The French were unsuccessful in their attempts to drive the English from the Hudson Bay territory and in 1713 they ceded their claims under the Treaty of Utrecht, which formally recognized British ownership of land surrounding the bay. The British had greater financial resources and would go on to pursue westward expansion, opening their earliest routes in the late eighteenth century.

Below: *The Pilgrims gathering wood for fuel in their first, harsh winter. They were ill prepared for life in the New World, and many succumbed to starvation.*

The English Colonies

In the 1600s and 1700s, the English colonies dotted the Atlantic coast from Massachusetts in the north to Georgia in the south. In their continued search for land, the colonists and their descendants encroached steadily upon lands from the Eastern Seaboard to the Mississippi River Valley and eventually to the

West, making—and breaking—treaties and alliances wherever they went.

The early English colonies comprised four basic groups: the Pilgrims and Puritans of Massachusetts, the Virginians of the Chesapeake Bay area, the Quakers of Delaware and eastern Pennsylvania, and migrants to the backwoods regions on the fringes of newly settled territory.

> *"Your principal end is not gain, nor glory, but to obtain souls to the glory of God."*
>
> —JOHN DONNE, 1622

The Pilgrims and the Puritans came from England as dissenters from the established religion. They, in turn, were intolerant of any deviation from their scrupulous observation of Biblically based tenets and customs. Their views precluded feelings of equality with or respect for the ways of the natives, who were regarded as heathen who must be converted and "saved." The tribes whose territory they settled on were New England Algonquian, including the Narragansett, Mohegan, Pequot, and Wampanoag, the latter of whom were initially helpful and friendly toward white settlers, teaching them about indigenous food and shelter-making. However, by 1620, when the Puritans arrived at Massachusetts Bay, local tribes had already been weakened by European diseases. Within a few years, they would realize that the newcomers were ruthless in their pursuit of both land and converts. One of the earliest allies of the Pilgrims was Massasoit, the Wampanoag grand sachem (chief), who had some acquaintance with early English traders. However, his sons, Metacomet and Wamsutta, grew up to distrust the invaders. Witnessing the ways of the English, Metacomet warned: "Brothers, these people from the unknown world will cut down our groves, spoil our hunting and planting grounds, and drive us and our children from the graves of our fathers, and our council fires, and enslave our women and children." The Puritan massacres carried out against the Pequots in 1637 made it clear that peaceful coexistence would be impossible.

Above: *Captain Myles Standish (center), a professional soldier and the Pilgrims' military advisor to (later leader of) Plymouth Colony, leading his brethren—with the help of a local guide.*

When Governor William Berkeley reached Virginia in February of 1642, the Jamestown colony there comprised some 8,000 people. More interested in trade than conversion, they had been on reasonably good terms with the Powhatan confederacy from 1607 until 1622, partly as a result of the conversion of Chief Powhatan's daughter Pocahontas and her tragically brief marriage to settler John Rolfe (she died of smallpox at the age of twenty-one). The Virginia Colony prospered during Berkeley's tenure as governor (to 1677). Its population grew from 8,000 to 40,000, and Berkeley played a part in creating a governing elite, whom he called "men of as good families as any subjects in England." This society persisted, as evidenced in the remarks of an Englishman in Virginia in 1724:

The habits, life, customs, computations of the Virginians are much the same as about London, which they esteem their home. For the most part, [they] have contemptible notions of country places in England and Scotland, whose language and manners are strange to them. They live in the same manner, dress after the same fashion, and behave themselves exactly as the gentry in London.

Most immigrants, however, came from the lower ranks of English society. More than 75 percent of those who came to the Virginia colony were young indentured servants: three out of four were youths between the ages of fifteen and twenty-four. The Virginia community was more rural than the Massachusetts Puritans. There were fewer skilled craftsmen, merchants,

ally included a profound contempt for other spiritual views. After 1642, Governor Berkeley passed laws that required "all nonconformists to depart the colony with all convenience." The Quakers (Society of Friends) had left England for Virginia and the mid-Atlantic colonies as a result of religious persecution. They were banished from Virginia in 1658, and Anglicans who were "loving to Quakers" were censured. It was a strange commentary on those who professed universal love as a tenet of their faith.

The Quakers' egalitarian values and belief in the "inner life" or spirit of God in every person distinguished them from the other colonists in that their attitude toward others—including native Americans—was less dismissive. The Friends repudiated violence completely and showed a measure of respect for the tribes they encountered, often seeking to alleviate distress without forcing their culture and beliefs on those they assisted. The principal area of Quaker settlement was an area granted to William Penn by royal charter in 1680, forming most of present-day Pennsylvania.

Two years after receiving the charter, Penn signed a treaty of friendship with the Lenapes (Delaware Algonquians)—the first treaty native Americans ever signed with colonial settlers.

and educators. The founders of Virginia shared the religious concerns of their day, at least nominally. John Donne, poet dean of St. Paul's Cathedral, preached a sermon to departing planters in 1622 that included the words:

Your principal end is not gain, nor glory, but to obtain souls to the glory of God. This seals the great seal, this justifies itself, this authorizes authority, and gives power to strength itself. You shall have made this island, which is but the Suburbs of the old world, a Bridge, a Gallery to the new; to join all to that world that shall never grow old, the kingdom of heaven.

Unfortunately, the zeal for spreading Christianity, as with other European colonists, usu-

Below: *A 1585 view of Pomeiock, a town in Florida, organized around a central communal fire. Some of the houses were covered with tree bark.*

Above: *Tobacco production was one of the most profitable ventures in the colonies. This illustration (c. 1670) is the earliest known depiction of an American tobacco factory, at a Quaker settlement in Pennsylvania.*

Unlike previous colonists, the Quakers regarded native rights to their lands and freedom of religion as issues to be considered seriously. By the time of these negotiations, the Lenape attitude toward the 1626 Manhattan Purchase—in which the island of Manhattan was "sold" to Dutch colonists for trinkets and tools worth approximately twenty-five dollars—was summed up by their saying: "The great white man wanted only a little, little land, on which to raise greens for their soup, only as much as a bullock's hide would cover. Here we first saw his deceitful spirit." Penn, by contrast, conducted the treaty meetings in good faith, attempting to define and protect the rights of his neighbors (who were represented by Tamanend, a chief after whom Tammany Hall was named).

The relative tolerance and liberality of Penn's Great Charter and Frame of Government for the colony soon attracted settlers not only from the British Isles, but from Germany, Scandinavia, and France as well. As Penn observed in *Fruits of Solitude* (1698):

> *Would God this Divine Virtue [Charity] were more implanted and diffused among Mankind, the Pretenders to Christianity especially, and we should certainly mind Piety more than Controversy, and exercise Love and Compassion instead of Censuring and Persecuting one another in any Manner whatsoever.*

Ironically, in 1734 Penn's own descendant, Thomas Penn, perpetrated one of the most infamous acts of fraud in the history of colonial-native relations, known as the "Walking Purchase." In need of funds to settle debts, he

> "*This very ground that is under me was my land and inheritance, and is taken from me by fraud.*"
>
> —LENAPE, 1737

The Visitors Settle In

Left: William Penn signing the historic treaty of friendship with the Lenape—the first to be signed by settlers and native Americans.

Left: The Quakers, shown here at a meeting, distinguished themselves from other colonists by their tolerance toward other religious beliefs—including native faiths.

Above: *Quakers journeying to a meeting across the snow in horse-drawn sleighs, as illustrated in this engraving from Sutcliffe's* Travel in Some Parts of America *(1811).*

Opposite: *Samuel Occum, a Mahican converted to Christianity, looking every inch the preacher.*

cheated the Lenapes at the Forks of the Delaware River into giving up their lands on the basis of a dubious (probably forged) deed that set boundaries based on "the lands a man can walk in a day and a half." Penn arranged for a path to be cleared through the rough underbrush and selected his fittest men to run as far as they could, defining a huge area of central Pennsylvania that effectively dispossessed the Forks group and their neighbors.

Beginning early in the eighteenth century, migrants to the eastern frontier areas comprised many Scots and Irish freeholders seeking land and a better life for themselves. They left behind rapacious landlords, high taxes, poverty, and oppression of various kinds. As land became scarcer in the colonized East, occupied by the emerging upper classes, these immigrants moved deeper into the forests, crossing the Appalachians to open another frontier. In so doing, they displaced still more of the native peoples. The result, inevitably, was growing enmity and strife: Although land was the principal issue at stake, the clash of cultural values caused further friction even where the colonists' motives were relatively benign.

British efforts to bring education and religion to native children were, not surprisingly, received with suspicion. As a rule, native children were loved and cared for by their families, and their education was undertaken by the entire tribe, passing on skills and mores by example and oral tradition. The English, on the other hand, sent their children away to school and used physical punishment as a means of instilling discipline. The Onondaga (Iroquois) orator Canassatego expressed this ethos in a 1744 address:

> *We love our Children too well to send them so great a way, and the Indians are not inclined to give their Children learning. We allow it to be good, and we thank you for your Invitation; but our Customs differing from yours you will be so good as to excuse us.*

Of all the English settlers, the Massachusetts Puritans were the most determined to "save" Indian souls and educate natives into white culture. Their methods were harsh, as their Calvinist doctrine incorporated the concept of original sin: goodness had to be beaten into children. Calvinist missionaries saw native cultures as pagan, if not demonic. Since God rewarded his followers with "externall beneficence and advancement as well as spirituall grace and blessings," the natives should be eager to embrace Christianity. In fact, the Massachusetts Bay Colony seal depicted an Indian crying out, "Come over and help us."

In the eyes of native Americans, the benefits of Christianity were far from obvious. As James Axtell observed in *The Invasion Within*, those who accepted baptism often died shortly thereafter—probably of white diseases. The Christian preoccupation with the afterlife and rejection of the present repudiated their own lifeways; in short, the Puritan ethic was strange, even hostile, to them. One native inquired of a missionary why they should pray to the Christian God when "our Corne is as good as yours, and we take more pleasure than you." In 1714 Experience Mayhew, a fourth-generation missionary, delivered a sermon on the "mysteries of religion" to the Mahicans at present-day New London, Connecticut. Following a session of attempting to answer the questions of his audience, Mayhew lamented that: "[they] could not see That men were ever the better for being Christians, for the English that were Christians would cheat the Indians of their Land and otherwise wrong them, and that their knowledge of books made them the more Cunning to Cheat others, & so did more hurt than good."

Cotton Mather, the Massachusetts Puritan minister who was instrumental in initiating the Salem Witch Trials of 1692, showed considerably less insight into native suspicion of Christianity when, in 1721, he expressed pained surprise at their disinterest:

Tho' they saw a People Arrive among them, who were Clothed in Habits of much more Comfort & Splendour, than what there was to be seen in the Rough Skins with which they hardly covered themselves; and who had Houses full of Good Things, vastly outshining their squalid and dark Wigwams; And they saw this People Replenishing their Fields, with Trees and

Contest of Cultures

Among the English colonists were a number of educators who—probably acting with the highest of motives—were determined to "civilize" their native charges. One such was Eleazar Wheelock, a minister and educator who founded "Moor's Charity School" for native Americans in Connecticut in the late 1740s. The inspiration for this venture was his success with his protégé, the Mahican Samuel Occum, who had enrolled at his school for young white gentlemen. Samuel Occum was eager to help his people, and his patron caught his enthusiasm.

The following letter to Wheelock is from his Indian student Hezekiah Calvin, a Mahican raised in Connecticut. He entered Moor's Charity School in April 1757, was approved as a Connecticut schoolmaster in 1765, and went to Fort Hunter, New York, to teach among the Mohawks. By 1767 his health had begun to fail, possibly due to the alcoholism against which he struggled throughout his short life. The letter expresses his confusion about the two worlds that he is trying to reconcile:

[Worthy Sir]:
After my most humble Dutys to you expressed, these are to let you understand that I am in a great [conflict]. I seem as if I wanted to go up among the Indians, & try to do them some good as far as it lays in [my] Power, and I want to go home, too, to see my Friends & relatives once more this Side Eternity (ie) if they are in the land of the Living. I think I shall never try to see that Country no more, if I could but only see my Parents this time. And if I should go up among the Mohawks, I shall feel quite uneasy until I do go home, But I leave the Matter with Mr. Wheelock & so ask Leave to Subscribe myself, Your Humble Pupil.

Shortly thereafter, Calvin wrote to his mentor again in the same ambivalent vein, with even more emphasis on his loneliness:

Reverend Doctor:
There is something that makes me want to go home, what, I cant tell, Home is in my Mind all the time. I want to go Home soon & see my Relations, & it seems to me to Tarry home a while or all the Time, & let me see if that I am able to support myself....I am uneasy while I am here & think upon home.

The last we hear of Calvin, then in poor health, is a condescending reference from Wheelock himself who wrote: "I hear that poor Hezekiah Calvin has got into Prison at Littleease for forging a pass for a Negro, & that it is probable he will fare badly. I hope God will humble him & do him Good by it."

with Grains, and useful Animals, which until now they had been wholly Strangers to; yet they did not seem touch'd in the least with any Ambition to come at such Desireable Circumstances, or with any Curiosity to enquire after the Religion that was attended with them.

Colonial Warfare

In the years between 1600 and 1800, Europeans and natives made war on each other, formed alliances, kept the peace, and made war again. Borders were drawn and redrawn. The most significant fighting took place in Virginia, between colonists and the Powhatan Confederacy; in New England, in the Pequot War and King Philip's War; and in northern New England and the Quebec region in the French and Indian War. The Revolutionary War would also involve natives. While the English and French fought to acquire territory, the losers were the natives, whose populations and tribal lands were drastically diminished.

Jamestown and the Powhatan Confederacy

Captain John Smith and his Jamestown colony benefited from their relationship with the Powhatan Confederacy. When the English established their colony in 1607, Powhatan (whose name was Wahunsonacock—he was called Powhatan by the English after the name of his tribe) controlled an alliance of thirty-two tribes and roughly 200 villages. Fewer than 20 percent of the initial 900 settlers survived their first three years in Jamestown. Without peaceful relations with the natives and practical help in overcoming malnutrition, the colony would have disappeared.

> *"Why will you take by force what you may obtain by love?"*
> — POWHATAN, 1609

Below: *New England Puritans braving the winter cold to attend church.*

Left: *John Eliot, a Puritan minister and New England's chief missionary to the native Americans, translated the entire text of the Bible into the Algonquian language; it was the first Bible published in North America.*

Below: *Theodor De Bry's engraving of the custom of planting arrows with locks of hair in the ground as a formal declaration of war for some tribes.*

The legend whereby John Smith was saved by Pocahontas (Matoaka), the chief's daughter, was probably exaggerated by Smith to enhance his reputation. It has been suggested that the event Smith described, in which she saved him from execution by her father, may have been part of an adoption ceremony unfamiliar to Smith.

From the beginning, dealings between Smith and Powhatan were relatively cordial, yet wary. Smith recorded an exchange with Powhatan in 1609:

Why will you take by force what you may obtain by love? Why will you destroy us who supply you with food? What can you get by war?…We are unarmed, and willing to give you what you ask, if you come in a friendly manner.…Take away your guns and swords, the cause of all our jealousy, or you may die in the same manner.

Powhatan did not destroy the Jamestown settlement: Peace was preserved until his death in 1618, although natives and colonists did not form a close bond. Powhatan's brother Opechancanough, who succeeded him as

Right: Robert Vaughan's engraving from John Smith's Generall Historie *(1624) of Powhatan in his royal tipi. "Before a fire upon a seat like a bedstead, he sat covered with a great robe, made of raccoon skins, and all the tails hanging by," Smith described after his first meeting with the great chief—although this artist evidently preferred to stick with his own vision of the "naked savages."*

leader of the confederacy, pursued an aggressive policy to oust the colonists. Early in 1622, when an English planter disappeared, settlers promptly retaliated by taking the life of a warrior. On Good Friday, according to the account of a Jamestown colonist, the Indians visited several settlements on the James River:

As at other times [they] came unarmed into our houses with Deere, Turkies, Fish, Fruits, and other provisions to sell us, yea in some places sat downe at breakfast with our peo-ple, whom immediately with their owne tooles [they] slew most barbarously, not spar-ing either age or sex, man woman or childe, so sudden in their execution, that few or none discerned the weapon or blow that brought them to destruction.

By day's end, 347 settlers, one-third of the colony, had died. An English militia was organized in response, and Governor Francis Wyatt proclaimed a new Indian policy: "It is infi-nitely better to have no heathen among us, who were but as thornes in our sides, than to be at peace and league with them....With our small and sicklie forces we have discomforted the Indians round about us, burnt their houses, gathered their corn and slain not a few; though they are as swift as Roebucks, like the violent lightning they are gone as soon as perceived, and not to be destroyed but by surprise or famine."

Battles between the colonists and natives occurred intermittently for the next two decades, until 1646, when peace was finally concluded with Opechancanough's successor, Necotowance. The Virginia Assembly set

C.Smith taketh the King of Pamavnkee prisoner 1608

Above and left: *The* Generall Historie *(1624) catalogued Captain John Smith's adventures in Virginia, with engravings illustrating Smith's narrative. Above, Smith is shown battling with warriors of the Pamaunkee tribe, 1607, before being taken captive (sketched in the background). Two years later, Smith takes the tribal chief prisoner.*

Right: *Pocahantas, Powhatan's daughter, who had converted to Christianity and been baptized into the Church, shown in a 1616 portrait.*

Below: *A colonist's view of natives of an unknown tribe returning from battle and presenting war trophies— including a human scalp— to their chief. Such images perpetuated the settlers' image of the barbaric nature of native Americans.*

boundaries and passed laws making it illegal for either group to venture into the other's territory uninvited. But the peace was uneasy, and minor skirmishing continued for generations.

Strife in New England

Between 1634 and 1676, the New England colonies engaged in two major conflicts, the Pequot War and King Philip's War. The Pequot War (1634–38) was engendered by leaders of the Massachusetts Bay Colony to gain control of the Connecticut Valley. The Pequots held the balance of power in the region. When a group of Pequots was alleged in 1636 to have killed John Oldham, an English trader, near Block Island, an avenging army was sent out under John Endecott. Several Pequot and Narragansett villages were attacked. The war escalated when the Pequot leader Sassacus raided Fort Saybrook.

Early in May 1637, an army of Englishmen and several hundred Narragansett and Niantic allies, led by captains John Mason and John Underhill, surrounded Sassacus's fortified village on the Mystic River, from which most of the able-bodied men were absent. The raiders set fire to the village. More than 600 people, most of them women and children, either died by fire or "were received and entertained with the point of the sword," as they tried to escape. Captain John Underhill recorded the slaughter:

> *Down fell men, women, and children. Those that escaped us fell into the hands of the Indians that were in the rear of us. Great and doleful was the bloody sight to the view of young soldiers who had never been in war to see so many souls lie gasping on the ground, so thick in some places, that you could hardly pass along.*

Underhill nevertheless tried to justify the massacre: "We had sufficient light from the word of God for our proceedings." Survivors were sold into slavery in the Caribbean or given as slaves to the allied tribes. The Pequots were forced to sign a treaty dissolving them as an autonomous people, and soon even the use of their name was outlawed.

King Philip's War, the only major Indian War of the seventeenth century, was so called after the English name for Metacomet, a son of the Wampanoag leader Massasoit. Metacomet believed that the colonists were responsible for the mysterious death of his brother, Wamsutta. He wanted to organize an alliance with other New England tribes against the English, whose continued presence had by now led to considerable resentment. As the most prominent of the New England chiefs, it was Metacomet who was summoned by the English to sign a peace treaty in Plymouth in 1671, in response to rumors of impending war.

Tension rose until fighting broke out in the Battle of Pocasset Swamp, fought July 19, 1675. Increase Mather (father of Cotton Mather) wrote an account of the battle, in which he observed that:

The Swamp was so boggy and thick of bushes, as that it was judged to proceed further therein would be but to throw away Men's lives. It could not there be descerned who were English and who the Indians. Our Men when in that hideous place if they did but see a Bush stir would fire presently, whereby 'tis verily feared, that they did sometimes unhappily shoot English men instead of Indians.

Several such battles took place in Wampanoag, Nipmuc, and Narragansett territory during the later months of 1675. Benjamin Church, an English commander, used information provided by his scouts to attempt to outwit his enemies. He reported two crucial factors in the native tactics that were identified by his informants:

Above and below: *Atrocities committed by the warring parties during the fighting at Narrangansett, 1637.*

Captivity Narratives

Between 1680 and 1716, captivity narratives were a popular form of frontier literature that continued well into the nineteenth century. Both natives and the colonists took captives, for a variety of reasons. Captives were adopted into many tribes primarily to help fill ranks depleted by warfare and disease, while the settlers, augmented by increasing birth rates and new immigrants, often took Indians captive to ransom their relatives. One of the most famous captivity stories was that of Minister John Williams of Deerfield, Massachusetts, who was taken to Quebec by Iroquois captors under French orders.

In spite of the opinions of many like Reverend William Smith of Philadelphia, who wrote confidently that there was no comparison between the advantages of a "primitive" life and those of "civilization," other observers disagreed. One of them was Benjamin Franklin, an incisive commentator on colonial life, who wrote:

> *When an Indian Child has been brought up among us, taught our language and habituated to our Customs, yet if he goes to see his relations and make one Indian Ramble with them, there is no persuading him ever to return. [But] when white persons of either sex have been taken prisoners young by the Indians, and lived a while among them, tho' ransomed by their Friends, and treated with all imaginable tenderness to prevail with them to stay among the English, yet in a Short time they become disgusted with our manner of life, and the care and pains that are necessary to support it, and take the first good Opportunity of escaping again into the Woods, from whence there is no reclaiming them.*

Having nothing to do except bring water and collect wood for cooking, I had some leisure which I occupied in hunting with a bow and arrow, the use of which I became quite expert, frequently shooting birds and at one time killing a fine rabbit, which I bore to the cabin with no small degree of pride....

Often in the long winter evenings, [I] listened with much pleasure and sometimes with deep interest to Cooh-coo-cheeh, as she told of the bloody battles of her nation, particularly with the Americans; of the great prowess of her ancestors; their chivalrous exploits, and "deeds of noble daring."

Oliver's father finally secured his release, but the boy was deeply affected upon parting from Cooh-coo-cheeh: "She spoke of the happiness of my family, especially the joy of my mother at my safe return; then of her own regret in parting with me, having, as she said, begun to regard me as her child; and concluded by saying that if I should grow up to be a man I must come and see her."

Not all captives were so fortunate as Oliver. In 1758, a young settler named Mary Jemison lost her entire family to a raiding party of six Shawnee and four Frenchmen. When they reached a Seneca camp, she was delivered to the household of two young women. According to her account: "During my adoption, I sat motionless, nearly terrified to death at the appearance and actions of the company, expecting every moment to suffer death. I was, however, happily disappointed, when at the close of the ceremony my sisters went about employing every means for my consolation and comfort. Being now settled and provided with a home, I was employed in nursing the children, and doing light work about the house." Some time later, she took a Seneca husband and spent the rest of her life with the tribe. She was one of many whom her contemporaries called "white Indians."

The attractions of a life of hunting and fishing were not lost upon ten-year-old Oliver Spencer, taken captive by Shawnee raiders in 1792. His parents had recently settled near the outskirts of Cincinnati, Ohio. While returning home alone from a party, young Oliver was detained by a party of warriors and led away without violence. He was taken to an elderly woman named Cooh-coo-cheeh, with whom he lived for some time. Writing of his experiences after he returned, he recalled:

The Indians always took care in their Marches and fights, not to come too thick together. But the English always kept in a heap together, that it was as easy to hit them as to hit an House. [The second factor] was, that if at any time they discovered a company of English Souldiers in the Woods, they knew that there was all, for the English never scattered; but the Indians always divided and scattered.

The English carried out a strategy of attrition, for which the loosely organized tribes were unprepared. Metacomet was killed in 1676. King Philip's War had cost the lives of perhaps 1,000 Englishmen and 3,000 native Americans.

The French and Indian War

By the mid-eighteenth century, both French and British colonists were firmly entrenched. Confrontation between them was inevitable, as each sought to dominate the "new" continent; it was also inevitable that each side would enlist natives as its allies, to fight their battles and exploit native knowledge of the terrain and the enemy. The Algonquians, including the Abenaki, Ojibwa, and Ottawa tribes, had close trading ties with the French and fought with them against the British, whose allies were Iroquoian.

> "Brethren, the Governor of Virginia and the Governor of Canada are both quarrelling about lands which belong to us."
> — HENDRICK (TIYANOGA), 1754

On the eve of the war, New York governor Clinton had offended the Mohawk leader Hendrick (Tiyanoga), who left Albany in anger. When the news reached London, Clinton's superiors were dismayed. To cement an alliance, they sent William Johnson, a trader and agent who was married to Molly Brant, sister of the Mohawk leader Joseph Brant (Thayendanegea). He came to Hendrick with gifts, promises, and

Sauvages Tchaktas matachez en Guerriers qui portent des chevelure

Right: *An eighteenth century sketch of a Choctaw family, a peaceful Muskogean-speaking tribe who lived in present-day Mississippi. During the colonial period, the Choctaws became embroiled in wars against the Spanish (resisting de Soto's expeditionary force); with the French against the English; and with the Americans against the British during the Revolutionary War.*

an invitation to the Albany Congress of 1754, which was accepted. Hendrick addressed the congress on July 2, 1754:

Brethren, you have asked us the reason of our living in this dispersed manner. The reason is your neglecting us for these three years past. You have…disregarded us; whereas the French [use] their utmost endeavors to seduce and bring our people over to them.…

Brethren, the Governor of Virginia and the Governor of Canada are both Quarrelling about lands which belong to us; and such a quarrel as this may end in our destruction…. It is very true, as you told us, that the clouds hang heavy over us….But we give you this belt [peace symbol] to clear away all clouds, that we may all live in bright sunshine, and keep together in strict union and friendship.

At first the war went badly for the British. Their commander, General Edward Braddock, was routed at Fort Duquesne (Pittsburgh) on July 9, 1755. One survivor of the engagement was the newly commissioned George Washington, who said of his Mohawk allies: "They are more serviceable than twice their number of white men. If they return to their nation, no words can tell how much they will be missed."

By October 1758, the war had turned in favor of the English, who were forging alliances with

more Iroquoian tribes. The war ended with British victory in 1760. The only apparent advantage the native allies gained from the war was the Royal Proclamation Act of 1763, which put all unceded lands under protection of the Crown.

> ## "*It is important for us, my brothers, that we exterminate from our land this nation which seeks only to kill us.*"
>
> —PONTIAC, 1763

There was much resentment against the British on the part of those native Americans who had been allies—now unrewarded for their participation in the fighting. In 1763 Pontiac, the Ottawa chief, led an alliance of Great Lakes Algonquians against the British. Pontiac's Rebellion, as it was known, achieved the reconquest of several forts captured by the British during the French and Indian War, but dissolved when the soldiers were deliberately infected by the British with smallpox.

"Between Two Hells"

In April 1775, the Revolutionary War between Great Britain and her colonists began. As a result of the Royal Proclamation Act of 1763, under which only the British Crown could settle land disputes, some natives felt that their interests lay with the British, who were now their nominal protectors; others sided with the colonists.

Joseph Brant was received by George III in 1776, and he pledged to solicit Iroquois support, contingent upon boundary violations being "settled to our satisfaction whenever the troubles in America end." A council of the Iroquois Confederacy was held at Oswego, on Lake Ontario, where Brant persuaded four of the six Iroquois nations to fight on the British side. The Oneida and Tuscarora, who did not attend the council, took the colonists' side, and the confederacy was split.

Throughout the six years of the war, atrocities were committed by all the combatants. Skillful in guerrilla warfare, the natives had an advantage much beyond their numbers and weaponry. Brant's men wiped out settlements in New York, Pennsylvania, Ohio, and Kentucky. However, the British suffered one defeat after the other at the hands of colonial troops. After the Treaty of Paris that ended the war in 1783, native Americans would contend with a new republic, which soon looked west for new territory to settle. In a conversation with his brother-in-law, William Johnson, Brant said despairingly: "We are…as it were, between two hells."

A radical change in social evolution would increase the pressure. The industrial revolution, well underway in Europe, would speed up the process of western migration by giving settlers the ability to overwhelm the native population in only a few decades with the help of railroads, steamships, repeating firearms, and other technological advances.

In 1784 the young U.S. Government signed its first native American treaty at Fort Stanwix, New York. The terms of the treaty were deeply resented. That year Joseph Brant, refusing to be conquered, led a thousand Iroquois loyalists north of the U.S. border to make a stand.

In the century to come, many native Americans would look to Canada, still under British rule, as "Grandmother's Country"—a reference to Queen Victoria. Several chiefs, including Sitting Bull, would lead their people north for survival. However, Canada would not prove an adequate refuge for native people who wanted to maintain their accustomed ways of life. There, too, the buffalo were being hunted out and the railroads making their disruptive incursions.

Left: Henry Knox served with distinction in the Revolutionary War and helped save Boston from the British in 1775 when he transported artillery to the besieged city from Fort Ticonderoga. He was appointed secretary of war in 1785, a position that he held until 1794, making him one of the chief architects of the new "hell" for native Americans.

Below: The mass exodus of an entire village exiled under the new removal policy to designated Indian territory in the West.

Westward Expansion

"Shall we, without a struggle, give up our homes, our lands, bequeathed to us by the Great Spirit?"

—TECUMSEH, 1811

Opposite: *Geronimo, revered war chief of the Chiricahuas, photographed in 1886, after his surrender to American troops. His violent resistance to the white man began in earnest in 1858, when his mother, wife, and children were viciously slain in their home by Mexican troops.*

Below: *Entitled "Pioneers of America," this engraving from the illustrated* Star Spangled Banner *presents an idealized view of frontier life.*

Even before it was officially formed, the nascent United States was expanding beyond its original borders. The Iroquois Confederacy had called the Atlantic colonies the Thirteen Council Fires: that number would steadily increase throughout the nineteenth century.

The population was growing, and land speculators sought out new territory east of the Mississippi for their ventures.

Losing Ground

The Shawnee chief Tecumseh fought to prevent westward expansion before and during the War of 1812 with Great Britain. In 1811 he traveled down the Wabash River to form a confederacy of disparate tribes, exhorting them:

Where today are the Pequot? Where are the Narragansett, the Mohican, the Pocanet, and other powerful tribes of our people? They have vanished before the avarice and oppression of the white man, as snow before the summer sun. Will we let ourselves be destroyed in our turn, without making an effort worthy of our race? Shall we, without a struggle, give up our homes, our lands, bequeathed to us by the Great Spirit? The graves of our dead and everything that is dear and sacred to us? I know you will say to me, "Never! Never!" Sleep no longer, O Choctaws and Chickasaws, in false security and delusive hopes.

After months spent fighting on the British side against the Americans, Tecumseh returned home to find his village burned. He mourned

the fact that "I could not induce them to come where the water turns to stone and the rain comes from the clouds in showers of white wool and buries everything in sight. I had to shut my eyes all the way so as not to see the beautiful country that would soon be trampled under the feet of the hated white men."

TECUMSEH.

Tecumseh was killed the following year in Canada, at the Battle of the Thames. He had never believed the claim made by Thomas Jefferson that the two races would merge peacefully and spread together across the continent. He understood that the Americans would push on until his people were displaced. Other leaders continued the resistance movement, including the Sauk warrior Black Hawk, who had also allied himself with the British. On a visit to his family in what is now Illinois (1813), he described the contrast between European and native warfare:

Instead of stealing upon each other, and taking every advantage to kill the enemy and save their own people, as we do, they march out, in open daylight, and fight, regardless of the number of warriors they may lose! After the battle is over, they retire to feast, and drink wine, as if nothing had happened; after which, they make a statement in writing, of what they have done — each party

claiming the victory! and neither giving an account of half the number that have been killed on their own side.

Willful ignorance on the part of Americans did almost as much damage as outright combat. In 1820 Colonel Hugh Brady came to Sault Ste. Marie, in present-day Michigan, to build a fort and cut down a clump of mountain ash sacred to the indigenous Ojibwa. Neengay, the wife of a white man, took on the role of peacemaker, telling her kinsmen: "The soldiers do not know Indians, my brothers. They mean well but are ignorant of our ways. Our ancestral votive tree is gone—by fire from heaven; by the ax of a new people. Its fall may be a symbol. The might of my people is ended; this I have long known. Accept it, my brothers! Let us live in peace."

While native populations declined, the white population rose steadily, assisted by immigration. Until late in the century, most immigrants came from northwestern Europe. Among the most numerous were Irish people fleeing the potato famines (from 1845) and Germans drawn by the prospect of farmland. Increasingly, these immigrants migrated west, along with groups fleeing religious persecution, like the Mormons, and, after 1848, would-be gold miners. The California Gold Rush brought some 370,000 adventurers from many different countries in search of easy wealth. Few found it, but they stayed on to become farmers, ranchers and merchants.

Before 1850 only one-third of what is now the continental United States had been transferred from natives to settlers—a process that took two hundred years. The vast majority of present-day Canada remained undisturbed, occupied by the native nations that had become established over the millennia since the crossing from Siberia. But from the 1840s onward, most of the American West came under U.S. control within a few decades. In Canada, population pressure due to westward migration did not become a serious problem until later, due to the vast extent of the territory, the relative scarcity of non-native settlers, and the rigors of the terrain.

> *"The might of my people is ended; this I have long known."*
>
> —Neengay, Ojibwa, 1820

After the Civil War, new pioneers set out on the Oregon Trail to rebuild their lives and prosperity. Civil War veterans like William T. Sherman took an active part in the Indian wars. Between 1778 and 1871, the federal government would make more than 300 treaties, not one of which was honored. In March 1871, an obscure rider to an Indian appropriation bill made such treaties with native tribes illegal. From then on, nebulous "agreements" and exploitative laws dominated government-tribal relations.

Right: *After the Homestead Act of 1862, Americans flocked west to claim land for cultivation. These emigrants homesteaded in Nebraska.*

Below: *A scene depicted by Charles Russell in which a Mandan villager tries to rub off the skin color of York, an African-American member of the Lewis and Clark expedition. After encountering the explorers, one Flathead noted: "One of the strange men was black. He had painted himself in charcoal, my people thought.... Those who had been brave and fearless, the victorious ones in battle, painted themselves in charcoal."*

As settlers continued to pour into the West, the native peoples made last-ditch efforts to preserve their ways of life. They realized now that they were wholly outnumbered: the best they could hope for was to maintain the integrity of their traditional folkways. New technology made this increasingly difficult. Their enemies included the transcontinental railway; the rapid-fire Gatling gun, used in 1890 at Wounded Knee; the French minié ball, which could kill at half a mile and was accurate up to 250 yards; and the repeating rifles and pistols carried by U.S. troops and local militia.

In one sense, the war for the American West began in 1804 with the expedition of Meriwether Lewis and William Clark, commissioned by President Thomas Jefferson to cross the continent, making maps and recording information on wildlife and plants. The government wanted knowledge of the tribes west of the Mississippi, and Jefferson enjoined the explorers to "treat them in the most friendly and conciliatory manner which their conduct will admit." Traveling up the Missouri in 1804, the explorers wintered in North Dakota, where they met Sacagawea, the Shoshone wife of a French trapper. She served as interpreter throughout the expedition, which continued up the Missouri, crossed the

Rocky Mountains, and explored the Columbia River. In showing that it was possible to cross the continent, Lewis and Clark opened the way for widespread settlement west of the Mississippi. Later, other explorers commissioned by the federal government would add to the knowledge about the West and its desirability as a source of land, game, gold, and timber. Men like Zebulon Pike, Charles Frémont, and Major Stephen H. Long were instrumental in increasing the pressure on tribes in the Northwest and present-day California, Nevada, Wyoming, Utah, and the Plains states—among the last areas to be settled, because they were popularly regarded as the "Great American Desert," as Pike described them after his travels in 1805–07.

The nomadic hunting tribes fared worst of all in the face of American expansion. Land agreements with stationary, agricultural tribes were at least comprehensible to the Americans in terms of the concept of the right to own property. In 1802 John Quincy Adams said,

Left: *President James Monroe, who helped negotiate the Louisiana Purchase. "The hunter or savage state requires a greater extent of territory to sustain it, than is compatible with the progress and just claims of civilized life…and must yield to it," he declared in 1817, the year he took office.*

Left: *A nomadic Sioux village in Wyoming, a home on land that settlers would soon claim.*

"[The] cultivated fields; their constructed habitations [are] undoubtedly by the laws of nature theirs.…But what is the right of the huntsman to the forest of a thousand miles over which he has accidentally ranged in quest of prey?" President Monroe echoed Adams's sentiment when he wrote in 1817: "The hunter or savage state requires a greater extent of territory to sustain it, than is compatible with the progress and just claims of civilized life…and must yield to it." The native American concept of the land as mother and provider, communally occupied rather than formally divided up and owned, was simply not grasped, either by governments or by individual settlers.

> "*What is the right of the huntsman to the forest of a thousand miles over which he has accidentally ranged in quest of prey?*"
> — JOHN QUINCY ADAMS, 1802

Waves of settlement continued to break across the Ohio River Valley and the Great Lakes region, especially after the War of 1812. Some soldiers were paid in land warrants instead of cash, and land agents sought homesteads for them along the Illinois and Wabash Rivers. The indigenous Kickapoo and Winnebago of northern Illinois fought back sporadically during the 1820s, but one Upper Country chief made a sustained effort to drive out the invaders in the face of broken treaties, tricks, and bribery: Sauk leader Black Hawk.

War, Resistance, and Removal in the East
The Black Hawk War broke out in 1832, when the Sauk returned from their new territory across the Mississippi to the village of Saukenek and refused to leave it. A federal force sent to the village in May dishonored a flag of truce and shot three Sauk warriors. Black Hawk's force of forty overcame an assault by almost three hun-

Seneca Orators

Two powerful spokesmen for the Seneca played a major part in the Iroquois League: Cornplanter (above) and Red Jacket, whose tribal name (Sagoyewatha) meant He Keeps Them Awake. They were rivals who differed in their approach to the Americans. Cornplanter favored concessions; Red Jacket was a strict traditionalist, especially opposed to European religion. In 1805 a preacher from the Evangelical Missionary Society of Massachusetts told the Seneca that "You have never worshipped the Great Spirit in a manner acceptable to Him; but have all your lives been in great error and darkness." Red Jacket replied: "If there is but one religion, why do you white people differ so much about it?"

Cornplanter, for his part, told the Seneca: "If we do not sell them the land, the whites will take it away." After terrorizing the frontier as a British ally during the Revolution, he pursued a peacemaking policy and eventually became a prosperous farmer on 1,300 acres in Pennsylvania.

dred militiamen, but federal and state troops were sent to hound the Sauk across Illinois and Wisconsin. At the Bad Axe River, some 300 Sauk men, women, and children were massacred by 1,300 troops on August 2, 1832. The Winnebago betrayed Black Hawk and other Sauk survivors to the authorities, who forced them to cede a strip of land fifty miles wide the length of present-day Iowa's Mississippi border. Before he was put on display in a series of eastern cities, the captured chief addressed government officials at Prairie du Chien, Wisconsin:

> *You have taken me prisoner with all my warriors. I am much grieved for I expected, if I did not defeat you, to hold out much longer and give you more trouble before I surrendered. [Black Hawk] is now a prisoner of the white man; they will do with him as they wish. But he can stand torture, and he is not afraid of death. He is no coward. Black Hawk is an Indian.*
>
> *We looked up to the Great Spirit. We went to our great father [the president]. We were encouraged. His council gave us fair words and big promises but we got no satisfaction.*
>
> *Things were growing worse.... We called a great council and built a large fire. The*

Sequoyah's Syllabary

A native of Arkansas, the Cherokee Sequoyah (c.1770–1843) grew up with a deep fascination for the "talking leaves" that the English used to communicate in written form. As a result, he became the only individual in history known to have developed an alphabet for a language with no written tradition. Beginning in about 1809, Sequoyah neglected his farm and his family to formulate a written language for the Cherokee tongue. First he experimented with pictographs, then with symbols for the syllables of the language. His completed syllabary contained eighty-six letters, and with it Sequoyah taught his tribe to read and write. His system was soon adopted for use in other native American languages, giving the indigenous peoples an advantage they had never enjoyed before. A brilliant young Cherokee named Elias Boudinot raised funds for a printing press with Sequoyan type, and in 1828 *The Cherokee Phoenix* began publication. Its "talking leaves" reached a wide readership and had a major influence on contemporary views.

spirits of our fathers arose and spoke to us to avenge our wrongs or die. We all spoke before the council fire. It was warm and pleasant. We set up the war whoop and dug up the tomahawk; our knives were ready, and the heart of Black Hawk swelled high in his bosom when he led his warriors into battle. He is satisfied. He will go to the world of the spirits contented. He has done his duty. His father will meet him there and commend him.

Like the Sauk, the other Algonquian-language tribes of the Great Lakes region were systematically displaced. They had sided with the French during the French and Indian War; some had joined Pontiac's Rebellion; most had been allies of the British during the Revolutionary War. Resistance to American settlement in the region was fierce and sustained. Potawatomi spokesman Metea addressed delegates to a treaty signing in 1821, when five million acres on the east side of Lake Michigan were finally ceded to the U.S. government:

> My Father: a long time has passed since first we came upon our lands; and our people have all sunk into their graves. They had sense. We are all young and foolish and do not wish to do anything that they would not approve, were they living. We are fearful we shall offend their spirits if we sell our lands; and we are fearful we shall offend you if we do not sell them.
>
> My Father, our country was given us by the Great Spirit, who gave it to us to hunt upon, to make our cornfields upon, to live upon, and to make our beds upon when we die. And he would never forgive us should we now bargain it away. When you first spoke to us for lands at St. Mary's, we said we had a little and agreed to sell you a piece of it, but we told

you we could spare you no more. Now you ask us again. You are never satisfied.

The Potowatomi, once thriving groups of buffalo hunters and forest hunter-gatherers, were eventually dispersed to locations as far-flung as Kansas, Oklahoma, and Mexico.

Removal was systematic in early nineteenth-century America. In President Andrew Jackson's first annual message to Congress (December 1829), he demanded a formal policy for the removal of all the native nations west of the Mississippi:

> There is no constitutional, conventional, or legal provision which allows [the new states] less power over the Indians within their borders than is possessed by Maine or New York. Would the people of Maine permit the Penobscot tribe to erect an independent government within their State? And unless they did, would it not be the duty of the

"*We are fearful we shall offend [our ancestors'] spirits if we sell our lands.*"

—METEA, POTAWATOMI, 1821

Government to support them in resisting such a measure? Would the people of New York permit each remnant of the Six Nations within her borders to declare itself an independent people under the protection of the United States? Could the Indians establish a separate republic on each of their reservations in Ohio? And if they were so disposed, would it be the duty of this Government to protect them in the attempt?

Among Jackson's immediate targets for removal were the so-called Five Civilized Tribes of the Southeast, based in Alabama, Georgia, Tennessee, Arkansas, and Florida. As early as 1824, the U.S. government had created Forts Gibson and Towson in present-day Oklahoma (designated Indian Territory) to prepare for relocation of these tribes. That same year, Secretary of War John C. Calhoun had established, without Congressional authorization, the Office of Indian Affairs. Not until 1832 would this bureau be backed by creation of a federal Commissioner of Indian Affairs.

Jackson also urged the Creek tribe, whom he had fought during the War of 1812, to move west of the Mississippi. In 1829, Creek elder Speckled Snake advised his people:

When the white man had warmed himself at the Indian's fire, and had filled himself with the Indian's hominy, he became very large. He stopped not at the mountain tops, and his foot covered the plains and the valleys. His hands grasped the eastern and western seas. Then he became our Great Father. He loved his red children, but he said: "You must move a little farther, lest by accident I tread on you."

Now he says, "The land you live on is not yours. Go beyond the Mississippi; there is game; there you may remain while the grass grows and the rivers run." Will not our Great Father come there also?...Brothers! I have listened to a great many talks from our Great Father. But they always began and ended in this—"Get a little farther; you are too near me."

Below: *Bloodhounds were used by the U.S. Cavalry in Florida to attack and viciously subdue the Seminoles.*

Right: *A traditional mask of the Cherokee, now the most populous U.S. tribe, despite their treatment at the hands of successive governments.*

Below: *President Andrew Jackson signed the Indian Removal Act on May 28, 1830, forcing all natives east of the Mississippi River to leave their lands for unsettled territory in the West. Robert Lindneux's painting of the Trail of Tears depicts their terrible journey.*

Overleaf: *George Catlin's 1838 portrait of Osceola, the young Seminole chief, after his capture by General T.S. Jessup. Three months after being taken prisoner, Osceola died.*

Some legislators sought to defend native rights, including Senator Theodore Frelinghuysen of New Jersey, who spoke out strongly during debates on the Indian Removal Bill in April 1830: "God, in his providence, planted these tribes on this Western continent, so far as we know, before Great Britain herself had a political existence. I believe, sir, it is not now seriously denied that the Indians are men, endowed with kindred faculties and powers with ourselves; that they have a place in human sympathy, and are justly entitled to a share in the common bounties of a benignant Providence. And, with this conceded, I ask in what code of law of nations, or by what process of abstract deduction, their rights have been extinguished?"

John Ross was another unsuccessful advocate for the Five Civilized Tribes. One-eighth Cherokee by blood, and the member of a powerful Tennessee family, he became an agent to the Arkansas Cherokee before the War of 1812. In 1828 he was elected chief; but he could not prevail against the forces for removal. His wife would be one of 4,000 who died on what the Cherokee called the Trail of Tears to Indian Territory during the late 1830s.

After much debate in Congress, Jackson signed the Indian Removal Act in 1830. It provided for an exchange of lands with the Indians residing in any of the states or territories, and for their removal west of the Mississippi. Section 6 stated: "And be it further enacted, That it shall and may be

Women in Native American Society

"Where are your women?" asked Cherokee chief Outtacity on meeting a British delegation to treaty negotiations early in the eighteenth century. The British were at a loss: What could he mean? Their women did not involve themselves in military and government affairs. This was one of the major differences in the contest of cultures.

In their societies, native American women stood at the center of the great circle of life, revered and sometimes even feared. Their capacity to bring forth new life and to grow the crops and harvest the wild plants that sustained the community made them essential. They considered themselves "part of" rather than "dependent upon," which gave them a dignity of bearing and an endurance wholly unfamiliar to Europeans of the contact period. In many tribes, property was owned by the women. They took an active part in government among the Cherokees and the Iroquois; property and titles descended through the female line among the Iroquois, Pawnees, and Pueblo peoples.

Non-natives who became familiar with the indigenous cultures realized that their women had a position of equality and respect unknown to "civilized" societies, in which women were, in fact, entirely subservient through lack of power—legal, financial, and religious, as well as physical. For native American women, the demands of a life lived in close harmony with nature had their own rewards in terms of simplicity, community, fair division of labor, communal child rearing, and traditions that respected women. Creation stories gave them a central role, and they were entrusted with sacred ritual objects. Their domain included healing and priesthood. And whether she served as gardener, water bearer, gatherer, or keeper of the dwelling and domestic animals, the Indian woman was certain of her place in society and the honor that accrued to her clan through performance of her tasks. The humility (from *humilis*, rooted in the earth) of this way of life could look upon adversity and death with acceptance in the certainty that life would go on.

Native novelist Louise Erdrich, author of *The Beet Queen*, *Tracks*, and *Love Medicine*, speaks to this world view when she says: "What makes sense to me is that there is a spiritual life in the landscape, and there's an emotional life around you that includes other forms of life. You may be projecting some of your self into it, but what's wrong with that? That's a Western idea: that you're you and it's it. I think we're connected and however that's expressed, that's part of Native belief; that we are influenced and influence everything around us, down to the last stone."

lawful for the President to cause such tribe or nation to be protected, at their new residence, against all interruption or disturbance from any other tribe or nation of Indians, or from any other person or persons whatever." John Marshall, chief justice of the Supreme Court, found the act unconstitutional.

> ## "I ask in what code of law of nations, or by what process of abstract deduction, their rights have been extinguished?"
>
> — SENATOR THEODORE FRELINGHUYSEN, 1830

The Removal Act did not explicitly authorize the use of force, but the government did little or nothing to protect the tribes from state militias. Georgia had long wanted to be rid of Indian land titles, and in 1831 the Supreme Court ruled, in *Cherokee Nation vs. Georgia*, that the Cherokee were a domestic, dependent nation, not a foreign nation. Four years later some Cherokee leaders signed the treaty of New Echota, surrendering their lands east of the Mississippi and agreeing to move to Oklahoma. Other leaders, including Chief John Ross, would repudiate this treaty, whereby the Cherokee would receive 5 million dollars for their land in Georgia, but the process of removal was underway.

Against the wishes of many of their women leaders, Cherokee men had adopted a constitution in 1817 based on that of the United States, in which, among other things, women were disenfranchised. Thus the once-powerful Cherokee women had no official voice in the struggle to retain their lands. Nanyehi, whose English name was Nancy Ward, was the last Beloved Woman, or head of the Council of Women, which was disbanded under the new constitution. She spoke out against the plan for removal, arguing that:

Cherokee mothers do not wish to go to an unknown country. We have raised all of you on the land we now have, which God gave us to inhabit. We have understood that some of our children wish to go over the Mississippi, but this act…would be like destroying your mothers. We beg of you not to part with any more of our land, but keep it for our growing children.

Fortunately, she did not live to see the terrible winter of 1838–39, when her people were rounded up at gunpoint and forced into camps. Led by General Winfield Scott, U.S. Army troops drove some 15,000 Cherokee west through Georgia, Kentucky, Illinois, and Missouri. Short of rations and unprepared for severe winter weather, some 4,000 died on the way to Oklahoma.

> ## "It is sweet to die in one's native land and be buried by the margins of one's native stream."
>
> — TSALI, CHEROKEE, 1839

About 1,000 tribespeople escaped to remain in the Great Smoky Mountains of North Carolina. Among those who tried to escape was a shaman named Tsali, who killed a soldier to protect his wife. He was tied to a tree and left to die, requesting that his friend Euchela carry a message to his son, lost in the mountains: "I want you to find that boy, if he is not dead, and tell him the last words of his father were that he must never go beyond the Father of Waters but die in the land of his birth. It is sweet to die in one's native land and be buried by the margins of one's native stream."

Other members of the Five Civilized Tribes were subject to forcible removal, including the Choctaw, Chickasaw, and Seminole, who fought back under the leadership of Osceola. When the U.S. Army came to central Florida in 1834, he took to the swamps with his warriors and

Charles Dickens Meets a Choctaw Chief

In 1842 the popular English author Charles Dickens (above, surrounded by some of his characters) visited the United States and spoke freely with many native leaders, whom he admired. One of them was Pitchlynn, a Choctaw chief, whom he met on a trip down the Mississippi. He recorded their conversation in "American Notes for General Circulation":

He had been away from his home, west of the Mississippi, seventeen months; and was now returning. He had been chiefly at Washington on some negotiations pending between his Tribe and the Government, which were not settled yet (he said in a melancholy way), and he feared never would be: for what could a few poor Indians do against such well-skilled men of business as the whites? He had no love for Washington; tired of towns and cities very soon; and longed for the Forest and the Prairie. I asked him what he thought of Congress? He answered, with a smile, that it wanted dignity, in an Indian's eyes.

Above: *Despondency and apprehension mark the faces of the natives in this painting by Charles Russell as they discover the white man's first wagon trail across the prairie.*

Opposite, top: *The canopy of this 1850s wagon reads "Pike's Peak or Bust," reflecting the determination of gold seekers to find their fortune.*

Opposite, below: *The ambush of wagon trains—a relatively rare occurrence—was a risk exaggerated by artists of the 1850s, many of whom subscribed to the glamorized "men of destiny" myth.*

waged guerrilla warfare, abandoning guns and returning to bows and arrows so that they could hunt without being discovered. They raided government encampments and inflicted many casualties before Osceola was entrapped by a flag of truce in 1838 and imprisoned in South Carolina, where he died three months later. The Seminole Wars of resistance continued until 1842, despite the fact that some 4,000 tribespeople were removed to Indian Territory. Those who remained in Florida took refuge in the Everglades and the Big Cypress Swamp, where their descendants live to this day.

"They could not capture me except under a white flag. They cannot hold me except with a chain."

— OSCEOLA, SEMINOLE, 1838

During Andrew Jackson's two terms in office (1829–37), ninety-four Indian treaties had been concluded under coercion. They included the treaty signed by the Sioux, Sauk, and Fox tribes in 1830, which gave the United States most of present-day Iowa, Missouri, and Minnesota and touched off the Black Hawk War.

Encroachment on the New Northwest

The longest and most arduous overland route across the continent had its origins in 1812–13, when explorer Robert Stuart traveled from the Astoria trading post in Oregon Country to New York City via Wyoming, Nebraska, and the Missouri River. The major tribes of the far Northwest included those of the Athapaskan, Salishan, and Penutian language groups along the Pacific Coast and, farther inland, the Nez Percé, Flathead, Bannock, Cayuse, and Kootenai nations. They were little disturbed by incursions from the East Coast until the late 1830s, when a major financial panic sent a wave of emigrants across America in search of a new start.

At that time, the Oregon Trail was 2,000 miles of hard travel by wagon train, and it was not until the 1840s that significant numbers of Easterners came into Oregon Country—roughly defined as the wilderness from northern California to Alaska and east as far as the Continental Divide. One journey made by a party of over a thousand people in 1843 became known as "The Great Emigration." Jesse Appleton, the leader of one column, wrote an account of the journey in which he described the "men of destiny" he led across the country:

No other race of men with means at their command would undertake so great a journey.... They have undertaken to perform, with slow-moving oxen, a journey of two thousand miles. The way lies over trackless wastes, wide and deep rivers, rugged and lofty mountains, and is beset with hostile savages.

Fears of Indian attacks on wagon trains were fueled by rumor and the reports and illustrations published in magazines like *Harper's Weekly*, which depicted women and children at the mercy of hostile warriors. Rebecca Ketcham, a schoolteacher, described feeling "very much afraid" during her westward journey after being told that "females were in very great danger of being taken by the Indians because they think a high ransom will be paid for them." Some letters and journals, however, also tell of nonhostile encounters, such as the account of Luella Fergus, who traveled west with her family as a young child in 1864. At an overnight stop, a group of Indians who had entered their camp saw Luella's mother pull out her false teeth. One observer, wrote Luella,

ran over to the other Indians, screaming and yelling, and they all took up the yell, leaving our camp in a hurry. A little later, they came back with a larger crowd and looked at Mother…[convinced] that she was a great prophet or witch. They were afraid and yet they wanted to see if mother would do the same thing again. She would not, however, and it was not long before they all pulled up and left us.

The fact that native Americans might have their own fears of hostile, violent encounters with emigrants did not concern those embarking on the westward trail. Most pioneers accepted the concept of Manifest Destiny: that the United States was inevitably bound for westward expansion, and the land was theirs for the taking. The Mormons believed they were journeying to the promised land: "This is a glorious way to come to Zion," declared one enthusiastic young woman as

Above: *The westward journey was a dangerous undertaking, and pioneers braved severely inclement weather, crippling lack of supplies, and their fears of hostile natives. Here, a wagon train carefully winds its way down a narrow trail.*

Like the journals of many travelers on the Oregon Trail, Appleton's account described the "trackless wastes" through which the wagons journeyed as uninhabited virgin wilderness. The "savages" were referred to merely as a threat akin to those posed by other hazards of the trail: wild animals, stormy weather, running out of food.

"*My heart fell down when I began to see dead buffalo scattered all over our beautiful country, killed and skinned, and left to rot by white men.*"

—PRETTY-SHIELD, CROW

she neared the end of her long, punishing journey on foot. Whether they traveled to escape poverty, slavery, or religious persecution, to seek their fortune in gold, or simply for a new start, the pioneers had little consciousness of the humanity of the native population, let alone of their rights to remain on their ancestral homelands.

News of the wagon trains was, however, received with fear and dread by the Plains and Northwestern tribes. "My heart fell down when I began to see dead buffalo scattered all over our beautiful country, killed and skinned, and left to rot by white men," recalled Pretty-Shield, a Crow woman, whose life story was recorded in her later years through an interpreter. Sarah Winnemucca, Paiute, described how terrified her family was on one occasion when "some white people were coming":

War and Pestilence!

HORRIBLE AND UNPARALELLED MASSACRE!

Left and below: Two typical nineteenth-century illustrations that contributed to pioneers' fears of Indian attacks during their westward journeys. "Almost any portrait that we see of an Indian, he is represented with tomahawk and scalping knife in hand, as if they possessed no other but a barbarous nature," wrote Tuscarora chief Elias Johnson in his history of the tribe, published in 1881. "Christian nations might with equal justice be always represented with cannon and balls, swords and pistols."

Everyone ran as best they could....My aunt overtook us, and she said to my mother: "Let us bury our girls, or we shall all be killed."...So they went to work and buried us, and told us if we heard any noise not to cry out, for if we did they would surely kill us...so our mothers buried me and my cousin, planted sage bushes over our faces to keep the sun from burning them.

During the early waves of emigration, both the United States and Great Britain claimed the Oregon region and had signed a joint occupation treaty in 1818. The U.S.-Canada boundary dispute would not be resolved until 1846, when Britain formally ceded Oregon Country. Meanwhile, growing numbers of settlers and miners were taking the Oregon Trail to seek their fortune in gold in California and, from 1850, along Oregon's Rogue River.

Canadian Expansion

Native-white relations had, on the whole, remained fairly amicable in Canada during the fur-trade era. Traders treated local tribespeople with a certain amount of respect and did not seek to cause hostility or seize lands for settlement. Some traders behaved fraudulently, even brutally on occasion, and most came with an apparently insatiable desire for native goods (primarily fur), bringing about changes to the economies and lifeways of the nations they encountered. The alcohol, disease, and dependency they brought were passed on without regard for the consequences, but also without malign intent. It was in the traders' interests to maintain the status quo: they needed a constant supply of goods and required the help and hospitality of local tribespeople to ensure their own survival.

Writing in 1880, H.B. Whipple, bishop of Minnesota, condemned in his preface to Helen Hunt Jackson's *A Century of Dishonor* the "sad revelation of broken faith, of violated treaties, and of inhuman deeds of violence" perpetrated by the United States against Indians. "Nations, like individuals, reap exactly what they sow; they who sow robbery reap robbery. The seed-sowing of iniquity replies in a harvest of blood," he wrote. By contrast:

All this while Canada has had no Indian wars. Our Government has expended for the Indians a hundred dollars to their one. They recognize, as we do, that the Indian has a possessory right to the soil. They purchase this right, as we do, by treaty; but their treaties are made with the Indian subjects of Her Majesty. They set aside a permanent reservation for them; they seldom remove Indians; they select agents of high character, who receive their appointments for life; they make fewer promises, but they fulfil them;...all their efforts are toward self-help and civilization.

Unfortunately, the bishop's observations were already long out-of-date by the time of his writing. Canada's westward expansion came later than the mass migrations in the United States; much of the territory of present-day Canada — including a substantial portion of the western region — was still relatively inaccessible and held no appeal for the settlers because of the climate and the inhospitable wilderness conditions of the terrain. By the mid-nineteenth century, however, "seeds of iniquity" were being sown north of the border that would inevitably result in a measure of death and dispossession for Canada's native nations, even if on a much lesser scale than in the United States.

Below: *A romanticized depiction of the "men of destiny" on their glorious journey across the wilderness.*

By the mid-nineteenth century, the non-native population of Canada was only about 3,250,000. In the East, that population dispersed slowly, primarily along the St. Lawrence River and into the Maritime Provinces. On the West Coast, Russian fur traders had been visiting Aleut communities east of the Bering Strait since the mid-eighteenth century. Some of their early incursions were bloody and brutal. Over a twenty-five year period the combination of murder and disease reduced the Aleut population by two-thirds. Farther south, new settlements among the Haida, Kwakiutl, Nootka, Tsimshian, and Coast Salish tribes spread out from a central area on southern Vancouver Island. Fewer than 20 percent of

A more hideous set of beings in the form of men and women I had never before seen. The fantastic manner in which many of the faces of the men were painted was probably intended to give them a ferocious appearance, and some groups looked really as if they had escaped from the dominions of Satan himself…. The women made, if possible, a still more frightful appearance. The ornament of wood which they wear to extend an incision made beneath the upper lip so distorts the face as to take from it almost the resemblance to the human; yet the privilege of wearing this ornament is not extended to the female slaves, who are prisoners taken in war. Hence it would seem that distinctive badges have their origin in the most rude state of society. It is difficult, however, for the imagination to conceive of more disgusting and filthy beings than these patrician dames.

Above and left: *Masks were an important part of the ceremonies of Pacific Northwestern tribes. Above, a Kwakiutl thunderbird; left, a Tsimshian war mask.*

Below: *Pioneers working together to overcome adversity. In Canada, waterways, rather than overland trails, formed the conduits for travel.*

the western settlers lived in communities of 2,500 of more, and their contact with the native tribes was minimal.

The traditional lifeways of these coastal tribes were disturbed relatively slowly by traders, explorers, and settlers, who ignored the natives or looked upon them with some curiosity — their salmon fishing, magnificent woodworking for housebuilding and seagoing canoes, and their ancestral rites, arts, and customs, including the potlatch, the ceremonial exchange of gifts that confirmed clan status and affirmed religious belief. Others were repulsed, as was Richard J. Cleveland, captain of an American trading vessel. In a narrative of his voyages, published in 1842, he described his impressions of the men and women he had seen in a Nootka village:

FIRST NATIONS — *Firsthand*

Right: A Nakoaktok elder, with facial piercing similar to that described so graphically in Captain Cleveland's journal, paints traditional decoration onto a hat.

Below: A typical Kwakiutl building in British Columbia, with intricately carved totem pole and tribal decoration painted onto the wood frame.

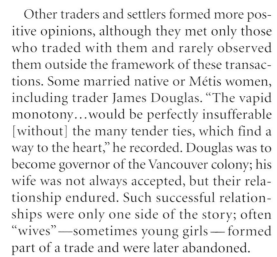

Other traders and settlers formed more positive opinions, although they met only those who traded with them and rarely observed them outside the framework of these transactions. Some married native or Métis women, including trader James Douglas. "The vapid monotony…would be perfectly insufferable [without] the many tender ties, which find a way to the heart," he recorded. Douglas was to become governor of the Vancouver colony; his wife was not always accepted, but their relationship endured. Such successful relationships were only one side of the story; often "wives"—sometimes young girls—formed part of a trade and were later abandoned.

Where more deliberate intrusion on the native nations of the coastal Pacific Northwest occurred, it was mostly by missionaries. One English preacher, William Duncan, was horrified by a Tsimshian tribe, and in particular, by his impressions of their practice of cannibalism. In 1857, the year he arrived in British Columbia, he recorded having seen:

> *a poor slave woman being murdered in cold blood, thrown on the beach and then torn to pieces and eaten by two naked savages.…O dreadful, dreadful to see one's fellow creatures like this when the blessed gospel has been 1800 years in the world.*

Duncan learned the language and gradually converted several Tsimshian villages, moving 600 people to form a new community farther north.

The interior of British Columbia, between the coastal mountains and the Rockies, was almost entirely populated by some 35,000 native people of several different language groups. The region had been explored by Captain James Cook in 1778, and by George Vancouver, Alexander MacKenzie, and Simon Fraser (who named it New Caledonia) in their fruitless search for the "Great White River"— the Columbia—between 1793 and 1808. All employed the help of native guides and all returned with reports of encounters, sometimes hostile, with warriors of local tribes along their expeditions, but their contact was limited to the transient experience of the passing explorer, almost a mutual curiosity.

With the discovery of gold in 1858 on the Fraser and Thompson Rivers came a rapid influx of prospectors, most of them American, some Chinese and European. The non-native population of Victoria, the English community on the southern tip of Vancouver Island, more than doubled overnight with the arrival on April 25 of a single ship from San Francisco carrying 450 goldseekers. Several months later, approximately 30,000 people had descended. "Never in the history of migrations of man has been seen such a rush so sudden and so vast," declared clergyman R.C. Lunden Brown.

"Never in the history of migrations of man has been seen such a rush so sudden and so vast."

—R.C. LUNDEN BROWN, 1858

The newcomers moved on rapidly toward the mining claims, creating such "instant" communities as Yale, Hope, and Lytton. Construction of the Cariboo Wagon Road, a 300-mile feat of high-level engineering from Fort Yale through the ravines and mountains of the interior, followed in the early 1860s.

Like their coastal counterparts, the native Dakelne, Nuxalk (Bella Coola), and Gitksan were shaken by the enmity of the new arrivals, with their unfamiliar diseases, alcohol, ethnic violence, and prostitution—and their proprietary attitude to the land they claimed. Missionary John Booth Good described Lytton as "a town which cannot be surpassed…[for] ungodliness, profanity, and vice." During the 1860s, smallpox raged up the Pacific coast from Victoria to Sitka, taking a toll as high as one in three in some Kwakiutl and coastal Salish communities. It devastated the Tlingit, many of whom had converted to Russian Orthodox Christianity during the fur-trade era.

Incursions also grew in the vast, sparsely inhabited interior of present-day Canada. Aside from the native population, the Métis, descendants of French fur traders and native women, lived for the most part in the Canadian plains region between Lake Superior and the Rockies, where, in the mid-nineteenth century, they outnumbered whites in the region by about ten times. The few communities occupied by both Métis and white settlers (most from the Hudson's Bay Company) included Red River, in what is now Manitoba. Tensions had flared up between these parties during the early part of the century, some of them developing into serious clashes, including the Selkirk incident (a battle over farmland) in 1816 and the Courthouse rebellion of 1849.

During the 1860s changes were occurring in Canadian politics that would permanently undermine the relatively peaceful (if mutually wary) relations among the native nations, Métis,

and white settlers: the Confederation movement was gaining strength. In 1860 the British government had transferred control over native affairs to Canada. Politicians of the United Provinces—roughly one-sixth of present-day Canada—were working for greater independence and grew increasingly apprehensive about American designs on western territory. In 1867, the same year that the United States purchased Alaska from Russia, the British Parliament passed the British North America Act, giving the new Dominion of Canada a constitution based on that of the United Kingdom. "Rupert's Land," a loosely defined area west of the Great Lakes, was purchased from the Hudson's Bay Company in 1868.

Below: *The arduous path in search of gold: miners ascending the challenging Chilkoot Pass.*

Canada's Waterways

Inland waterways played a vital part in the history of native North America, before and after European contact. The Eastern Woodlands people plied the region's many rivers and streams in lightweight birchbark-and-cedar canoes, used for travel, warfare, trading with other tribes, and carrying fish and game from the hunt. In Canada, inland waterways were the primary means of travel and transport, which often involved long portages around waterfalls and turbulent rapids. Europeans adopted the same routes for exploration and settlement: the Hudson and St. Lawrence rivers, the Great Lakes, and the countless waterways of the Ohio River system.

European exploration of northern North America was closely linked to the search for a Northwest Passage by water across the continent to Asia. The fur trade expanded west from Hudson's Bay to the Canadian North West on the river roads, and the Columbia River was identified by Lewis and Clark as the most important in the American West. Inevitably, the routes that had served the First Nations for hundreds of years became instrumental in their decline, as traders, soldiers, and settlers dispersed more widely across the continent.

British Canadians began to move west from Ontario in increasing numbers. In the Red River Valley, relations with the natives and Métis deteriorated quickly as more settlers arrived during the 1860s. The Métis culture was a blend of French Catholicism and native traditions, which set the group apart from both the settlers and natives. The latest (Protestant) newcomers were equally scornful of both Métis and native people and sought nothing less than the annexation of the entire region to the Dominion of Canada. An 1860 editorial in *The Nor'Wester*, the British-Canadian local newspaper, read:

The wise and prudent will be prepared to receive and benefit by the changes Ottawa would make whilst the indolent and careless, like the native tribes of the country, will fall back before the march of a superior intelligence.

Sir John Macdonald, Canada's first prime minister, sent a land surveying party to the Red River Valley in 1869. Louis Riel led the Métis opposition to the intruding surveyors, declaring: "The Canadian government had no right to make surveys in the Territory without the express permission of the people of the settle-

Left: *A Cree moose hunter blows his horn, imitating nature's call.*

Below: *A scene that symbolizes the expanding railroad system driving the buffalo from their roaming grounds to near-extinction.*

ment." The dispute, which became known as the first Riel Rebellion, escalated into armed conflict between the Canadians and an alliance of Métis, native, and mixed British-native groups. The revolt was suppressed, and Riel went into temporary exile in the United States.

> *"The Canadian government had no right to make surveys in the Territory without the express permission of the people of the settlement."*
>
> —LOUIS RIEL, 1869

In 1866 the mainland colony of British Columbia merged with the Vancouver colonists to form a new province. Its legislature, facing debt problems, immediately began to consider

Right: *A child equipped with snowshoes and thick fur clothing, attire developed for survival in the harsh subarctic winters.*

its status and economy. It debated options including a merger with the United States before agreeing, in 1871, to become a province of the Dominion of Canada—with the stipulation that the Canadians build a railroad link with eastern Canada. The laborious process of building the railroad across the western wilderness forms a long chapter in Canadian history. One bridge of the 600 constructed in British Columbia alone—across a canyon in the Selkirk Mountains—required 2,000,000 board feet of lumber. Snow slides and flooding were constant dangers. And as in the United States, land transfers were made arbitrarily: all land not specifically granted to individuals was considered government property.

By now, Canada's territory stretched across the continent from coast to coast. A flood of immigration from eastern Canada began, soon to be increased by the completion of the transcontinental Canadian Pacific Railroad in 1885, linking Halifax with Vancouver. During the railroad's epic construction, natives and Métis were displaced, pushed north and west. Many of Canada's new immigrants were settling in Manitoba, farming the fertile land.

Late in 1885, Riel and his Métis confederates sent a demand for the redress of grievances, including fair settlement of native claims, to Ottawa. When his petition was ignored there, Riel formed a provisional government. In the North West Rebellion of 1885, combined native and Métis bands attacked the Canadian Mounted Police, which had been formed to keep peace in the area in 1873. The Métis routed the "Mounties" at Duck Lake, near Prince Albert on the North Saskatchewan River, then overreached themselves by trying to enlist the area's major tribes in a general rebellion. The Blackfeet refused, but two bands of Cree joined Riel. The government responded by sending troops out on its new railway.

Riel's forces were defeated near Battleford, Saskatchewan, and Riel was hanged for treason. The leaders of his Cree allies, Big Bear and Poundmaker, were imprisoned for two years. Both died within six months of their release. French Canadians, who identified with the Métis, were incensed by the treatment of Riel. "At the moment when the corpse of Riel falls through the trap and twists in convulsions of

"Riel, our brother, is dead, victim of his devotion to the cause of the Métis."

—Honor Mercier, 1885

agony, at that moment an abyss will be dug that will separate Quebec from English-speaking Canada," warned one Quebec politician, J. Israel Tarte. Honoré Mercier, Quebec's Liberal leader, addressed a crowd within days of Riel's death with the forceful words:

Riel, our brother, is dead, victim of his devotion to the cause of the Métis, of whom he was the leader, victim of fanaticism and treason—of the fanaticism of Sir John [MacDonald] and some of his friends, of the treason of three of our people who sold their brother to keep their portfolios.

Unfortunately, within a few decades, the Canadian government had instituted the same repressive measures against the native people as their neighbors across the border. Competition for land did not reach the level it had in the United States, and there were fewer armed conflicts, but reservations were created and cultural and religious expressions banned in many places. The Plains Indian and Métis buffalo hunt was suppressed. The potlatch was outlawed in 1884, and religious artifacts were stolen by the police or destroyed by missionaries.

"They believed themselves to be the only inhabitants of the universe, and that all the rest of the world was a mass of ice."

— Scottish explorer, 1818

Eventually, even the nomadic people of the High Arctic found their lifeways changing under the impact of white influence. Most Arctic tribes had experienced little or no contact with people outside their own kin. During his 1818 expedition John Ross, a Scottish explorer, met an Inuit group in Greenland, of whom he said:

They exist in a corner of the world by far the most secluded which has yet been discovered....Until the moment of our arrival, they believed themselves to be the only inhabitants of the universe, and that all the rest of the world was a mass of ice.

A few years later, George Lyon, an English explorer in search of the Northwest Passage, found his vessel stranded in ice at the north

Below: A nomadic Inuit family outside their "tupik," a summer dwelling constructed with animal skins stretched over a frame of branches.

Right: Chief Joseph, a leader renowned for his insight, was a reflective diplomat as well as a warrior. "Good words do not last long until they amount to something. Good words will not give me back my children," he once said.

Right: Before the Mission era, the Maidu of California were hunter-gatherers. Here, a woman makes acorn mush, using the traditional method for removing the acorn's bitter taste.

end of Hudson Bay, but was rescued by the local Iglulik (Inuit), with whom the sailors remained trapped for two years. Having learned the language and lived under generous Iglulik hospitality, Lyon observed: "I verily believe that there does not exist a more honest set of people than the tribe with whom we had so long an acquaintance."

By the mid-nineteenth century, the growing demand for baleen—flexible whalebone used to make corset stays—brought whalers to the

Arctic and attracted the nomadic Inuit to their stations for trade and employment. Their acquisition of modern rifles led to overhunting of the caribou and seal they depended upon. Traditional skills and crafts were eroded by dependence on trade goods, just as they had been farther south.

Chief Joseph of the Nez Percé

South of the border, the Nez Percé leader Hinmaton-Yalakit, whose English name was Chief Joseph, led a foredoomed resistance to encroachment on his tribe's Wallowa Valley lands, where Oregon, Washington, and Idaho now meet. Elected chief of the Nez Percé in 1873, he inherited a forced treaty with the U.S. government, concluded in 1863, that required eviction of his tribe to Idaho. When the army arrived to enforce the treaty in 1877, led by General Oliver O. Howard, the Nez Percé began a 1700-mile retreat toward Canada, fighting thirteen engagements as they went. Fewer than a thousand of the Nez Percé—600 of them women and children—evaded ten army divisions before they were trapped at Bear Paw Mountain, Montana, only thirty miles from the Canadian border. Newspaper accounts of the tribe's determined resistance engendered widespread support for the Nez Percé.

When Chief Joseph finally surrendered his exhausted band, he summed up the tragedy of the native peoples when he said, "My heart is

sick and sad. From where the sun now stands, I will fight no more forever." The Nez Percé were imprisoned at Fort Leavenworth, Kansas, before being transported to the Quapan Agency in Indian Territory. Chief Joseph's former enemy, General Howard, worked with him to secure their return to the Wallowa Valley to no effect. Despite a personal appeal to President Theodore Roosevelt on a trip to Washington in 1877, the "Indian Napoleon," as he was called, lived out his days on Washington State's Colville Reservation, where he died in 1904.

California and the Southwest

In 1834 the Mexican government, newly independent of Spain, began to dismantle the oppressive mission system that had dominated the Chumash, Pomo, Salina, and other California tribes for more than a hundred years. Natives who had been baptized into Christianity, called neophytes, were supposed to benefit by the redistribution of land. More often, they ended up as poorly paid workers for landholders of Spanish descent, faring even worse than they had, without the mission food distribution to fall back on. "The Indians…do all the hard work, two or three being attached to each house," wrote Richard Henry Dana, Jr., in 1840, after visiting California. "And the poorest persons are able to keep one [servant], at least, for they have only to feed them and give them a small piece of coarse cloth." Traditional sources of wild plant food were disappearing, as horses, cows, and sheep introduced by the Spanish overgrazed the region and non-native crops crowded out indigenous plants. After the Mexican Cession of 1848, the United States took possession of California, whose native population was by then estimated at 150,000—half its pre-mission level.

Despite the harmful effect of the missions, the gold strikes at Sutter's Mill that year would bring even more sweeping change to the

region. Between 1848 and 1852, more than 175,000 settlers rushed to California, lured by the prospect of vast fortunes. This influx proved disastrous for the local Maidu, Miwok, and other tribes. The government aided volunteer groups to "clear out" villages for the new settlers. One victim described her experience during a brutal raid on her village:

They killed my grandfather and my mother and my father. I saw them do it. I was a big girl at that time. Then they killed my baby sister and cut her heart out and threw it in the brush where I ran and hid.…I was so scared that I guess I just hid there a long time with my little sister's heart in my hands.

At first local tribespeople were pressed into service as a cheap labor force to work the new mines, but, as machinery began to replace the need for laborers, they became expendable and were either driven away or simply killed. When the State of California was admitted to the Union in 1850, its newly installed governor authorized the militia to attack Indians, who were perceived as a threat to miners and immigrants. A law was passed to allow the indenture of native orphans or the children

Above: *Horses, introduced by the Spanish, were quickly adopted by Southwestern tribes and eventually became a symbol of the Old West.*

"*My heart is sick and sad. From where the sun now stands, I will fight no more forever.*"

—CHIEF JOSEPH, 1877

Above: *Two young Mojave tribesmen, posing in the 1870s for the now-famous lens of Timothy O'Sullivan.*

of consenting parents. This led to a brisk trade in kidnapped native children, whose parents were killed so the children could be sold to ranchers in the Central Valley.

The native population of California was reduced to an estimated 30,000 by 1870—now only one tenth of its pre-mission era level. In 1883 Helen Hunt Jackson, author of *A Century of Dishonor,* and Abbott Kinney submitted a report on the Southern California Mission Indians to the Commissioner of Indian Affairs. An extract from their opening summary reads:

Considerable numbers of these Indians are to be found on the outskirts of white settlements…where they live like gypsies in brush huts, here today, gone tomorrow, eking out a miserable existence by day work, the wages of which are too often spent for whiskey in the village saloons. Travellers in Southern California, who have formed their impressions *of the Mission Indians from these wretched wayside creatures, would be greatly surprised at the sight of some of the Indian villages in the mountain valleys, where, free from the contaminating influence of the white race, are industrious, peaceable communities, cultivating ground, keeping stock, carrying on their own simple manufactures of pottery, mats, baskets, etc., and making their living, a very poor living it is true; but they are independent and self respecting in it, and ask nothing at the hands of the United States Government now, except that it will protect them in the ownership of their lands—lands which, in many instances, have been in continuous occupation and cultivation by their ancestors….From tract after tract of such lands they have been driven out, year by year…until they can retreat no farther; some of their villages being literally in the last tillable spot on the desert's edge or in mountain fastnesses….*

The history of the thirteen years between the passing of the Secularization Act and the conquest of California is a record of shameful fraud and pillage, of which the Indians were the most hapless victims….With every year of our neglect the difficulties have increased and the wrongs have been multiplied. All that is left in our power is to make them some atonement.

Farther north, the Modoc tribe, led by Kintpuash (nicknamed Captain Jack), turned to armed resistance to reservation life during the 1870s. Pushed off their grasslands on the California/Oregon border in 1864, this small tribe of hunter-gatherers spent six years on a nearby Klamath reservation before returning to Lost River, where they wanted their own reservation. Local ranchers demanded their eviction. Eventually, the U.S. army and local militiamen set off the conflict known as the Modoc War. In 1873 the Modoc were driven from the lava beds where they had taken a stand against the army, and hunted down. Kintpuash and several of his confederates were hanged at Fort Klamath, after which they were decapitated; their embalmed heads were sent East and displayed in a touring carnival.

The Gold Rush

For most people, the phrase "Gold Rush" summons up the great 1849 migration to California that began with the discovery of gold at Sutter's Mill in 1848. Or the rich strike in the Alaskan Klondike that brought more than 100,000 hopefuls across the arduous mountain route to that remote region beginning in 1897. However, the western United States and Canada experienced a whole series of such discoveries over a period of decades, all of which brought bad news to the indigenous peoples.

In British Columbia, gold brought chaos to Vancouver Island, the Caribou region, and the Fraser River area during the latter half of the 1800s. Alaska's silent wilderness was disrupted by the discovery of a rich vein of gold in the Yukon in 1898. Similar strikes in Colorado, Idaho, and Dakota had similar results: an influx of strangers in the grip of "gold fever," with their attendant gambling tents, saloons, diseases, and shopkeepers charging what the market would bear. As the pictures on the right show, gold was recovered by various forms of placer mining in streambeds, where the heavy ore was deposited in "placers" by currents that washed it from the underlying bedrock. Panning for gold was a laborious process that might yield a few nuggets for hours or days of grueling work. Only a fortunate few of the men and women who rushed to the gold fields found riches.

Frustration bred by failure made murder a common occurrence in the gold camps. Natives and foreign immigrants were the usual targets. Rape was epidemic. In some areas, like southern California, native Americans were pressed into service as cheap minefield labor even as the plants and animals they lived on were hunted out and dispersed. Government treaties were trampled in the rush, as in western Dakota Territory, where gold was discovered in the sacred Black Hills in 1876. As in the days of first contact, gold proved to be an evil portent for the First Nations.

Above: *Looking out across the dangerous quicksand to the ruins of ancient Anasazi dwellings built into the formidable walls of Canyon de Chelly, Arizona.*

The Navajo and Apache Wars

The Navajo, who call themselves the Diné, are related to the Apache tribes of the Southwestern desert and mountains. The Navajo became a target of the U.S. Army during the 1840s, when they carried out livestock raids against settlers in their region, as they had long done against neighboring Pueblo tribes and Mexican settlers. By 1850, the tribe — today, the nation's largest — comprised some 12,000 members living in small kinship groups from the Rio Grande to the Grand Canyon. They herded sheep in the canyons and mesas of this region, which had remained relatively undisturbed until the 1850s, when a series of U.S. army posts was built in the area, including the stronghold at Fort Defiance, near Canyon de Chelly, Arizona.

The Navajo resented the infringement on their ancestral grazing grounds, and a series of attacks and counterattacks ended in a full-scale assault on Fort Defiance, which the army abandoned in 1860.

From 1861 on, the Navajo were subject to severe reprisals by the government, including widespread destruction of their crops and live-stock. A tenuous peace was established before the Civil War, but hostilities broke out again when Colonel Christopher "Kit" Carson renewed the campaign against Navajo home-steads and carried it into Canyon de Chelly itself. He was joined by Mexicans and several native groups that had suffered from Navajo raids, including the Ute and the Zuni. Chester Arthur, Navajo, wrote in his later account of the period:

Wingate and other army posts. Some months later, they were taken away to Bosque Redondo—an arid strip of land along New Mexico's Pecos River, reached on a 300-mile forced march called the Long Walk. Some 8,000 Navajo made the trip and spent four years in exile near Fort Sumner, undergoing many hardships. Their numbers were reduced by 25 percent by the time their chief, Manuelito, negotiated a treaty with the U.S. government in 1868 whereby they could return to their own country. A 3.5-million-acre reservation was set apart for them, contingent upon their keeping the peace, and they retained some 35,000 sheep and goats to re-establish their herds. Manuelito left a moving account of their return from exile:

When we saw the top of the mountain from Albuquerque we wondered if it was our mountain, and we felt like talking to the ground, we loved it so, and some of the old men and women cried with joy when they reached their homes.

Every day the Mexicans and the Utes would ride out over the country, and whenever they found sheep or pony tracks, they would follow them and kill the herders. The rich Navajos, who had many sheep and goats, drove them west as far as Oraibi, where the Hopi villages are, and many went so far they took refuge in the bottom of the Grand Canyon, but now from every side other Indians came in to fight them. Even the Paiutes and the Apaches had been given guns to kill them and chased them clear into the wild mountains. All their crops were destroyed and when winter came the people began to starve.

Petroglyphs on the walls of New Mexico's Largo Canyon depict the catastrophic campaign waged against the Navajo during the years 1863–64. Their hogans were destroyed, their orchards cut down, and some two million pounds of corn burned. Those who tried to hide in the caves of the canyon walls were hunted out and arrested. Some chose suicide by leaping from the cliffs, rather than face imprisonment. Finally, most of the Navajo nation was rounded up and interned at Fort

Left: *The Navajo are renowned for their skills and arts, particularly their weaving and silverware, as displayed by this 1880s trader.*

Left: *Nachez, son of Chiricahua Apache chief Cochise, with his wife.*

Several bands of Navajo fighters had evaded the U.S. Army troops and escaped the removal. They remained at large as renegades, living precariously in canyons and caves while their fellow Navajo endured the four-year exile at Fort Sumner. Manuelito, son of the prominent Navajo leader Cayetano, was a resourceful fighter who kept up his people's courage, vowing, "My God and my mother live in the west and I will not leave them." Another courageous leader was Barboncito, known as "the Orator," who had signed the ill-fated peace treaties of the 1840s. Ultimately, only the small band of Kayenta Navajo avoided capture or surrender: they had found freshwater springs in a secret canyon behind the top of Navajo Mountain, which enabled them to hold out until the rest of their people returned to Canyon de Chelly.

> *"My God and my mother live in the west and I will not leave them."*
>
> — MANUELITO, NAVAJO

An Abiding Fascination

Artist George Catlin, born in Wilkes-Barre, Pennsylvania, in 1796, began his career as a portrait painter in Philadelphia. Deeply impressed by a delegation of Indians on their way to Washington, D.C., he traveled west in the early 1830s to make a pictorial and written record of the native nations before their customs and lifeways were altered still further or erased entirely. He painted numerous portraits and tribal scenes in the Missouri River country, which he exhibited in Europe in 1840. During his travels, he became a strong supporter of Indian rights, recommending the creation of a great Western national park to preserve both regional tribes and the remnants of the buffalo herds that had sustained them.

In 1841 the prolific Catlin published *Manners, Customs, and Condition of the North American Indians* in two volumes, with some three hundred engravings. Two years later he published twenty-five plates entitled *Catlin's North American Indian Portfolio*. His last trips to the West, during the 1850s, were recorded in *My Life Among the Indians*. His books and paintings, including 470 full-length portraits of individuals and tribal scenes, form an invaluable record, much of which might have been lost except for his efforts. The greater part of his artwork went to the National Museum in Washington, D.C., while some seven hundred sketches were presented to the American Museum of Natural History in New York City.

At the same time as the Navajo Removal, Apache uprisings took place throughout Mexican territory that had been recently acquired through the Mexican War and the Gadsden Purchase of 1853. Like the Navajo, the Apache, who were nomadic mountain and desert dwellers, had a long history of raiding Mexican ranchers and pack trains on both sides of the border. Chiricahua Apache chief Cochise had allowed Americans to build a stagecoach line through southwestern New Mexico, with a way station in Apache Pass. However, violence erupted in 1861, when Cochise was wrongfully accused of cattle theft and kidnapping. Attempts to capture him under a flag of truce resulted in the Cochise War, in which the Chiricahua Apache leader was joined by his father-in-law, Chief Mangas Coloradas (Red Sleeves). Both soldiers and settlers were killed, and Apache Pass was closed to travelers bound for California for many months.

Nature's Rhythms

The Anasazi, or Old Ones, ancestors of the Pueblo peoples, inscribed this cross (symbolizing the four directions) in the Cave of Life, in Arizona's Petrified Forest. The cross is surrounded by fertility figures. For forty-five days before and after the winter solstice, a shaft of sunlight strikes the center of the cross. Near this site is a prehistoric stone carving of a mountain lion, and fragments of pottery show that small groups of farming Indians occupied northern Arizona more than a thousand years ago. Other remnants of these ancient cultures include shell jewelry and petroglyphs with a variety of Southwestern motifs: geometric designs, lizards, birds, spirals, zigzags, and star patterns, all derived from the natural world. Two other prominent symbols are the plumed serpent (representing rain) and the thunderbird, a powerful spiritual helper. The latter was worn as a patch by the 45th Infantry Division during World War II.

> *"I have drunk of these waters and they have cooled me; I do not want to leave here."*
>
> — Cochise, 1866

In 1862 Union soldiers drove Confederates from New Mexico and Arizona, then turned their howitzers on the Apache warriors. Mangas Coloradas was imprisoned at Fort McLane and reported killed when "trying to escape." Cochise took a stand in southern Arizona's Dragoon Mountains and renewed his raids on settlers. He and his warriors held out against the army after the Civil War, refusing to give in to demands during 1866 negotiations for the removal of the Chiricahua Apache to the Tularosa reservation. Cochise was, by now, desolate at the prospect of the loss of Apache autonomy. He pleaded for an alternative settlement:

I want to live in these mountains; I do not want to go to Tularosa. That is a long way off. The flies on those mountains eat out the eyes of the horses. The bad spirits live there. I have drunk of these waters and they have cooled me; I do not want to leave here.

Right: *Tom Torlino, Navajo,
photographed in 1882.*

Cochise fought for another six years, until he was forced to succumb to the promises of General George Crook for amnesty on federal reservations in 1872.

A relative peace reigned until the mid–1870s, when the Indian Bureau took control of the reservations at Camp Verde and Fort Apache and forced relocation of the Tonto and White Mountain Apaches to the arid San Carlos Valley, where farming was almost impossible. A band of warriors led by Goyathlay, called Geronimo, left the reserva-tion and fled to Mexico in 1882, pursued by General Crook. Geronimo's resistance lasted until the end of 1886, when he was deported with some of his men to St. Augustine, Florida, as prisoners of war. Even after their release, two years later the Chiricahua Apache were denied access to their homeland. They remained in custody at Fort Sill, Oklahoma, for nineteen years before the army appropri-ated their farms for use as an artillery range and relocated them to the Mescalero Apache Reservation in New Mexico.

"*My heart would ache for revenge...*"
— Goyathlay (Geronimo)

Geronimo was such a wily and elusive fighter that he came to be regarded with grudging admiration by his adversaries on both sides of the Mexican border. His legendary resolve to resist the "white man's invasion" of his territory had been cemented when he found, on returning from a trip in 1858, that his village had been attacked by Mexican troops. As he wrote in his autobiography:

When all were counted, I found that my aged mother, my young wife, and my three small children were among the slain. There were no lights in camp, so without being noticed, I silently turned away and stood by

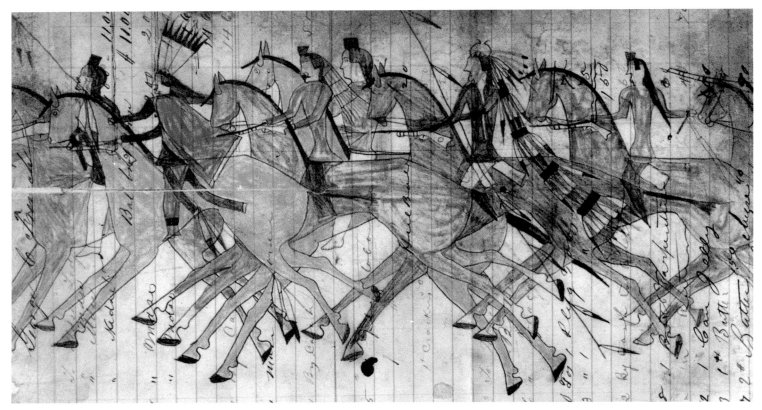

Ledger Art

By the 1860s, members of the Plains tribes had acquired ledger books from traders and were using them to tell their stories. Favorite subjects included warriors on horseback, fights between tribesmen and U.S. cavalrymen, and scenes from daily life. Ledger art was a continuation of traditional painting on tipis and other shelters, and of the pictographic "winter counts" recording the events of a given season. The acquisition of ledgers and other paper goods also brought new media, including ink, pencils, and watercolors, which would eventually replace traditional methods of painting—stick and bone brushes on hide.

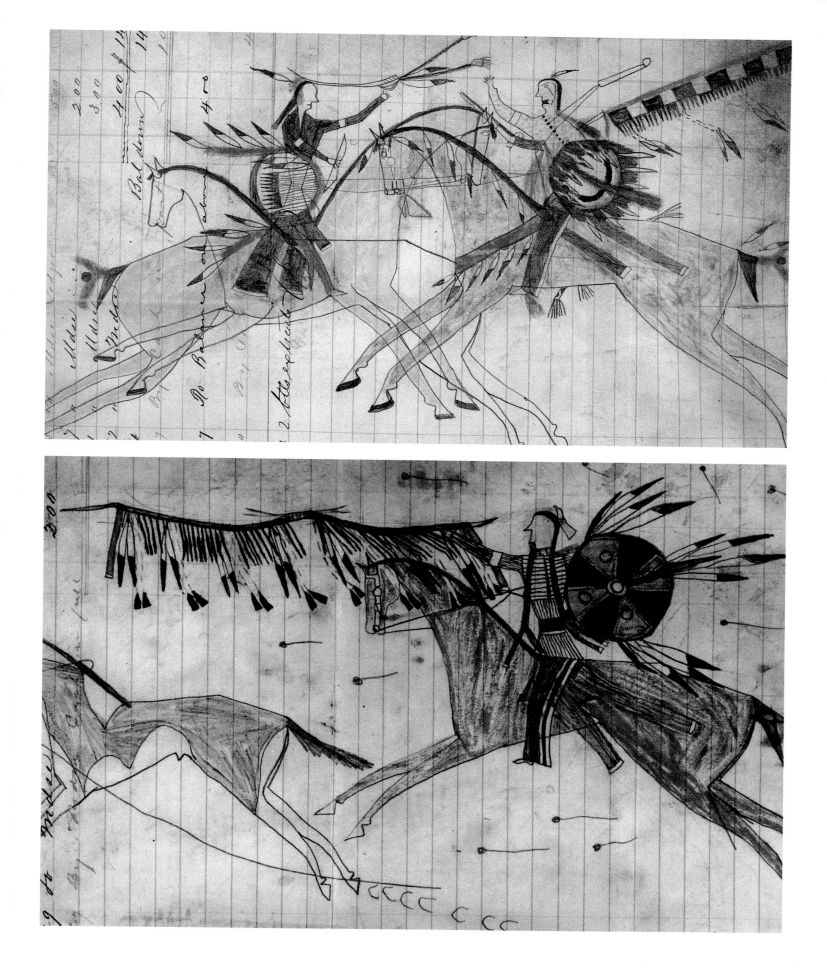

The Civil War and After

Native Americans took part in the Civil War for a variety of reasons, including poverty and lack of employment. By 1861 many tribes had become so dependent upon the surrounding community that they had to show their loyalty by participating, whether in Union or Confederate forces. In some cases, the institution of slavery had caused divisions within the tribe. This was true of the Oklahoma Cherokee: native leader Stand Watie, who became one of the last Confederate generals to surrender, owned slaves; other members of the tribe opposed slavery.

Union colonel William H. Emory benefited by the scouting skills of the Lenape (Delaware) who accompanied him into the western theater. Their leader, Black Beaver, warned him of the approach of a company of Texas Mounted Rifles, leading to the capture of their advance guard. The scouts then led the Union expedition 500 miles through enemy territory to Fort Leavenworth without incurring casualties.

In 1862 supplies promised the Dakota (Santee Sioux) by the U.S. government in return for lands in Minnesota were interrupted by the war. This triggered the rebellion known as the Minnesota Indian War, in which the Dakota killed or captured hundreds of settlers and half-blood Indians, whom they called "cuthairs." The rebellion was suppressed a year later, and thirty-eight Dakota were sentenced to death by hanging at Mankato—the largest mass execution in U.S. history.

After the war, many generals of both sides, including William T. Sherman (above), helped implement the 1867 "Peace Commission" plan to confine all the Great Plains natives on two reservations: northern tribes in the Black Hills of Dakota Territory and southern tribes in Indian Territory. The writing was now on the wall for the Plains tribes, for whom Sherman was one of the most aggressive enemies. "We have now selected and provided reservations for all," he said in September 1868. "All who cling to their old hunting grounds are hostile and will remain so till killed off." In a letter to his brother, U.S. Senator John Sherman, he expressed his murderous contempt even more explicitly:

The more we can kill this year, the less will have to be killed the next war, for the more I see of these Indians the more convinced I am that all have to be killed or maintained as a species of pauper. Their attempts at civilization are simply ridiculous.

the river....I stood until all had passed, hardly knowing what I would do. I did not pray, nor did I resolve to do anything in particular, for I had no purpose left....I was never again contented in our quiet home [and when I] saw anything to remind me of former happy days my heart would ache for revenge upon Mexico.

Geronimo's seasoned guerrilla fighters could survive on next to nothing while crossing the Rio Grande with impunity to raid ranches and homesteads in the old Apache style. He might have remained free indefinitely, had it not been for the final straw, the capture of women and children in his band in 1886. His three strongest warriors, including his half-brother, White Horse, chose to lay down their guns after the hostages were taken, and Geronimo agreed to follow them into custody.

After his release in 1892, still barred from Arizona, he accepted an invitation to share the Kiowa and Comanche reservation in Indian Territory, where he took up farming and joined

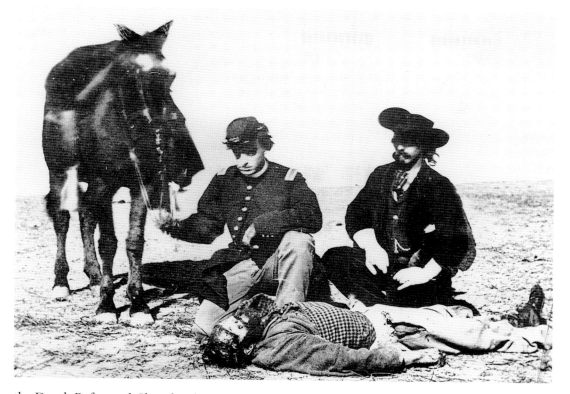

Left: *Scalped—the gruesome end most dreaded by soldiers fighting for the Plains. For many tribes, scalps were taken as trophies or to provide proof of the victim's death. Plains Indians also believed that people entered the "next world" in the form they took at the moment of death: enemies were often deprived of their eyes, hands, and teeth to deny them the corresponding functions.*

the Dutch Reformed Church. Then he toured for a year with a Wild West show, appearing in Omaha, Buffalo, New York, and the St. Louis World's Fair. Four years before his death, he was invited to Washington, D.C., by President Theodore Roosevelt to take part in the inaugural parade of 1905. He left a valuable record of his life and times in the 1888 autobiography, *Geronimo: His Own Story.* During World War II, his popular name became a jumping call for U.S. army paratroopers—another kind of immortality.

The Last West

Only after the West Coast was partially settled did pioneers look to the Great Plains and Great Basin areas, which became known as the "Last West." The Great Basin region remained inhospitable except to the Northern Paiute, Bannock, and Shoshone who hunted and gathered between the Rockies and the Sierra Nevada. Travelers on the California Trail called them "Diggers," since much of their sustenance came from wild roots. It was the Plains tribes who became synonymous with the term "American Indian" as the Last West fell before the railroad, buffalo and bounty hunters, miners, homesteaders, and the U.S. cavalry.

Major Plains tribes included the Cheyenne, Pawnee, Blackfeet Kiowa, Arapaho, and many Siouian-speaking groups, from the Dakota, or Santee Sioux of the upper Missouri in North Dakota, to the hunting tribes: Nakota, Lakota, Assiniboine, and Crow. In the southern plains were the Plains Apache, Shoshone, Comanche, Ute, and Kiowa.

The infamous Sand Creek, Colorado, massacre of a peaceful encampment of Cheyenne and Arapaho families in 1864 was the prelude to years of active resistance by allied Plains groups including the Cheyenne, Arapaho, and Sioux. At Sand Creek, tensions that had been growing since the 1858 discovery of gold in Cherry Creek erupted into violence. In the city of Denver, originally a mining camp, the bodies of a miner's family were laid out for public viewing as the victims of "savagery" by unspecified Indians. A so-called "Colorado Militia" of 700 ranchers, miners, and soldiers set out looking for vengeance, led by a former clergyman named John M. Chivington. On the morning of November 27, they found a peaceful encampment of Cheyenne and Arapaho troops under the protection of Chief Black Kettle, who had surrendered at Fort Lyon two months before. By the post com-

The Vanishing Buffalo

By the mid–1850s, millions of buffalo had been killed by white hunters for their thick pelts, which were made into warm coats. The slaughter increased during the Civil War as the demand for leather and robes increased. Plains tribes like the Kiowa, Sioux, and Blackfeet saw their way of life vanishing with the great animals whose bones were unceremoniously piled along railroad tracks and around waterholes where they had been slaughtered by repeating rifles. Most of the meat was left to spoil, although the tongues were considered a delicacy. By 1875, perhaps a million bison remained of the estimated 50 million that had roamed the Great Plains as late as 1870.

mander's orders, the encampment raised an American flag and a white flag, but the signal of peace was ignored by Colonel Chivington, who cried: "Kill them all, big and small!" In the ensuing carnage, 123 people were literally cut to pieces—100 of them women and children. Robert Bent, the son of a white trader and a Cherokee woman who accompanied Chivington as a guide, described the appalling brutality he witnessed:

I saw five squaws under a bank. When troops came up to them they ran out and showed their persons to let the soldiers know they were squaws and begged for mercy but the soldiers shot them all. I saw one squaw lying on a bank whose leg had been broken by a shell. A soldier came up to her with drawn sabre. She raised her arm to protect herself when he struck, breaking her arm…he left without killing her.…Some thirty or forty squaws…sent out a girl about six years old with a white flag on a stick. She was shot and killed.…I saw one squaw cut open with an unborn child lying by her side [and] quite a number of infants in arms killed by their mothers.

Other accounts were even more graphic. In his harrowing testimony given before Congress on his investigation into the massacre, Major Wynkoop reported: "Women and children were killed and scalped,…and all the bodies mutilated in the most horrible manner. The dead bodies of females profaned in such a manner that the recital is sickening, Colonel Chivington all the time inciting his troops to their diabolical outrages."

> ## "*His presence here is an insult and a threat.… I am for war!*"
> — RED CLOUD, 1866

Left: *Crazy Horse, Oglala Sioux, the legendary chief who first won distinction in Red Cloud's successful war against the Bozeman Trail in 1856–58. After marrying a Cheyenne woman, this skilled strategist formed a Sioux-Cheyenne resistance alliance, and went on to lead the Cheyenne, Arapaho, and Sioux in the successful 1876 attack against Custer's forces.*

The tragedy at Sand Creek, which became synonymous with gratuitous brutality, mobilized widespread hostility, both against native Americans and against the perpetrators of the massacre. East Coast abolitionists and other liberal-minded citizens spoke out on behalf of the victims, while native Americans were angered beyond appeasement and frontiersmen took a harder line against them than ever.

Perhaps the most hopeless struggle of all was that against the increasingly sophisticated new technology that settlers and miners brought to bear: the prairie windmill, which provided effective irrigation; and the steel plow used by the "sodbuster" to cut through the grasslands. The influx of goldseekers on the Bozeman Trail to Montana, which traversed the Sioux's Powder River hunting grounds, added further pressure. Oglala Sioux Chief Red Cloud defiantly retaliated, with the help of his strategist Crazy Horse. Red Cloud was a powerful orator. At the Powder River Council Fire in 1866 he energized his fighters with the exhortation:

Left: *Red Cloud, a Sioux chief, inspired his warriors with powerful rhetoric to fight against the encroaching whites.*

Above: *A delegation of native Americans in the 1870s, converging on the White House to pursue their issues with President Ulysses S. Grant— tactics that proved ineffective in putting an end to the bloodshed and dispossession.*

Hear ye, Dakotas! When the Great Father at Washington sent us his chief soldier [General Harney] to ask for a path through our hunting grounds, a way for his iron horse [railroad] to the mountains and the western sea, we were told they merely wished to pass through our country, not to tarry among us, but to seek for gold in the far West. Our old chiefs thought to show their friendship and good will when they allowed this dangerous snake in our midst. They promised to protect the wayfarers.

Yet before the ashes of the council fire are cold, the Great Father is building his forts among us. You have heard the sound of the white soldier's ax upon the Little Piney. His presence here is an insult and a threat.…I am for war!

The Sioux drew U.S. General William J. Fetterman from the safety of Fort Phil Kearny in Wyoming Territory and killed him and eighty cavalrymen in an ambush. The attack was as vicious as any seen on the Plains: soldiers were found stripped and scalped. Several of the bodies bristled with dozens of arrows. "I give you some of the facts as to my men, whose bodies were found at dark," read the official report prepared by Colonel Henry B. Harrington. "Eyes torn out and laid on rocks; noses cut off; ears cut off; chins hewn off; entrails taken out and exposed."

The coup at Fort Phil Kearny brought on government withdrawal from the Bozeman Trail and the last major peace treaty negotiations with the Plains Indians, in 1867–68. Some 5,000 southern Plains Indians attended the first session of the Fort Laramie treaties, held at Medicine Lodge Creek, Kansas, in 1867. Leaders present included Arapaho chief Little Raven; Kiowa warrior Satanto, called White Bear; half-blood Quanah, whose white mother had been a Comanche captive (who was surnamed Parker); and Yapparika Comanche Ten Bears, who spoke eloquently on behalf of peace. The agreement that resulted created two large reservations in Indian Territory:

one for the Kiowa and Comanche, the other for the Cheyenne and Arapaho. Native leaders agreed in principle to conform to the rules of reservation life, including church attendance, white-run schooling, subsidies of food staples and cattle, and an agricultural way of life entirely foreign to their culture.

In 1868 a second round of talks, with the northern Plains tribes, was held at Fort Laramie. On paper, it gave Chief Red Cloud most of what he had fought for, including designation of the Powder River Country (in present-day Wyoming and Montana) as "unceded Indian territory." In addition, the Great Sioux Reservation would include all of what is now South Dakota west of the Missouri River. These lands included the Black Hills sacred to other tribes including the Cheyenne, Kiowa, and Crow.

The Cheyenne and Arapaho soon had cause to regret their agreement to settle in Indian Territory. Broken promises and bootleg liquor resulted in livestock raids on Chickasaw and other reservation neighbors; then Cheyenne war parties attacked nearby settlements, killing at least eighty settlers and kidnapping several children. General Philip Sherman retaliated by sending the 7th Cavalry, led by the young lieutenant colonel George Armstrong Custer, against a quiet Cheyenne encampment on Oklahoma's Washita River. More than 100 Cheyenne were shot to death, including Chief Black Kettle and his wife, who had survived the Sand Creek massacre.

> ## "Whoever interferes will hear this gun."
> — LITTLE BIG MAN, 1876

Meanwhile, the Sioux were being invaded by miners and settlers seeking access to the Black Hills that had been declared off limits. By 1876, 6,000 had taken up residence in Custer City, South Dakota. Senate negotiators who came to Sioux territory seeking a lease agreement were met by impassive faces. Oglala Sioux Little Big Man, dressed for battle, led a chant that ended: "Whoever interferes will hear this gun."

In March 1876, General George Crook undertook a campaign against the last Plains Indians to rebel against the government. On the Rosebud River, on June 17, he unexpectedly encountered a huge encampment of Sioux, led by Crazy Horse, who forced him to retreat. Five days later, Lieutenant General George Custer led the 7th Cavalry to disaster on the east bank of the Little Bighorn River. Ranged against him were six tribes comprising the largest native gathering in the history of North America: Cheyenne, Sans Arcs, Miniconjoux Sioux, Oglala Sioux under Crazy Horse, Blackfeet, and Hunkpapa Sioux led by chiefs Sitting Bull and Gall.

Reprisals for "Custer's last stand" were swift and severe. The Indian Confederacy dissolved in the the face of increasing military pressure,

Below: *Daring, brilliant, sometimes considered a maverick, George Armstrong Custer was the youngest general in the Union Army when promoted to this rank at the age of twenty-three and, later, a lieutenant colonel in command. Because he staged raids on enemy camps before daylight, the Sioux called him "Son of the Morning Star."*

Right: *The battle of June 25, 1876, at Little Bighorn, popularly known as "Custer's last stand." Custer, blundering into the largest gathering of hostile tribes in Western history, unwisely divided his regiment into three columns. The allied fighters led by Crazy Horse and Chief Gall annihilated Custer and his men. Crazy Horse was hunted down, arrested and "eliminated" a year after the battle.*

and Sitting Bull took his remaining people north to Canada in 1877. Faced with starvation, and unaided by the Canadian government, they returned to North Dakota and surrendered at Fort Buford in 1881. Northern Cheyenne chiefs Little Wolf and Dull Knife, imprisoned on the Southern Cheyenne reservation, would lead a desperate flight from Indian Territory to join Red Cloud's people at the Pine Ridge Agency in 1878. They were intercepted just short of their goal, after evading soldiers and militiamen throughout the long trek north.

Wounded Knee

The Paiute medicine man Wovoka, whose name means The Woodcutter, was born in western Nevada about 1858. During the solar eclipse of January 1, 1889, Wovoka was suffering from a fever; he fell into a trancelike state and experienced a vision in which he moved among his ancestors in the afterlife. They told him to resist the white man and generate spir-

itual sustenance for this resistance among his people by means of the Ghost Dance, a ceremonial sacred dance.

Wovoka's "medicine"—the Ghost Dance religion—spread rapidly, while he himself became a living legend, reputed to be invulnerable to gunfire and able to bring rains in a drought. He preached nonviolence:

When your friends die you must not cry. You must not hurt anybody or do harm to anyone. You must not fight. Do right always....Do not tell the white people about this. [The savior] is now upon the earth. He appears like a cloud. The dead are all alive again. I do not know when they will be here; maybe this fall or in the spring. When the time comes there will be no more sickness and everyone will be young again. Do not refuse to work for the whites and do not make any trouble with them until you leave them. When the earth shakes [at the coming] do not be afraid. It will not hurt you.

The widespread popularity and strength of the Ghost Dance movement, with its subversive consequences, alarmed the white community, who attempted to discredit and harass Wovoka at every opportunity. The agitation surrounding the movement escalated; among the Lakota Sioux, whose morale had been miserably low, the dancing and visions provided hope as a means to bring their oppression to an end. Instead, in December 1890, the U.S. government sent troops into the reservations to quell the movement. At Pine Ridge Reservation, South Dakota, almost 300 people—many of them women and children—were gunned down by the 7th Cavalry on December 29, in another disgracefully brutal incident that had been triggered by an exchange between a soldier and a man who refused to turn over his weapons. A mass grave was dug on a nearby hill on New Year's Day: the Wounded Knee site remains a place of mourning for the Sioux.

Left: After Wovoka, Short Bull, Sioux, was perhaps the leading figure in the Ghost Dance movement.

Below: William T. Sherman and Sioux delegates met at Fort Laramie, Wyoming, in 1868, where they signed the short-lived treaty designating the Powder River Country as "unceded Indian territory."

Right: *Victims of the chillingly ruthless Wounded Knee massacre in their mass grave.*

Right: *Victims of the chillingly ruthless Wounded Knee massacre in their mass grave.*

An episode of gratuitous killing, the massacre was, in part, an act of revenge for the death of George Armstrong Custer at the Little Bighorn River. One of those killed was Chief Big Foot, who had met Custer in 1876 and advised him not to make his ill-advised foray into the Yellowstone River region. Wounded Knee, a crushing show of superior firepower and the intent to use it even against unarmed, peaceful peoples, proved the end of the Indian Wars period: the flame of resistance was finally extinguished.

The demographic map of North America had changed radically by 1890: the population of the United States was approximately 60 million, that of Canada close to 4 million. Between 1820 and 1870, some 7.5 million immigrants had come to the United States, most of them from northern and western Europe. The native peoples had been forced onto reservations (called reserves in Canada), and their combined numbers had reached a low point— fewer than 2.5 million.

After hostilities stopped, both the U.S. and Canadian governments continued their efforts to undermine native culture. Putting parents to work and sending their children away to boarding schools remained a policy. In 1883, a *Code of Religious Offenses* was issued by the Bureau of Indian Affairs. It designated most native American ceremonies crimes punishable by imprisonment. The sun dances of the Plains tribes were banned, as were the healing rites of medicine men and women. Traditional native practices like polygamy were outlawed, putting unmarried and widowed women at risk, as they would have no one to hunt for them. Also banned were the so-called animal dances, in which traditional costumes of fur or feathers were worn. Giveaway ceremonies, practiced by many tribes across the continent, and the potlatch of Northwest Coast peoples, were outlawed.

"We cannot go on living the life we once knew. We must begin a new life."
— CHIEF JOSEPH, NEZ PERCÉ

Left: *The aftermath of the slaughter in the canyon at Wounded Knee, a scene adding to the evidence that this was the most barbaric of battles.*

Below: *Big Foot, leader of the Sioux and a victim at Wounded Knee, frozen in the South Dakota snow.*

Reservations

"It may be that some little root of the sacred tree still lives."

—BLACK ELK, 1930

From the late nineteenth century until well into the twentieth, in both Canada and the United States, a legislative "war against Indianness" followed the end of the Indian Wars. Both countries enacted a series of laws that would deprive indigenous people of formal title to much of their remaining land. Apart from the seemingly insatiable demand of a burgeoning non-native population for more land, the governments were also influenced by the prevailing anthropological philosophy: that with help from their "civilized" brothers, native Americans could and should be "improved" and, ultimately, assimilated.

A Period of Transition
Legislators on both sides of the border believed that assimilating natives into mainstream culture was the answer to "The Indian Problem." Assimilation was also seen as the answer to Canada's Métis problem—the treatment of those people of mixed Indian-French descent who had developed a unique culture apart from Canadian and native society. It was

Opposite: Oglala Lakota women of Pine Ridge Reservation lining up to receive their beef ration from government employees. Reservation dwellers were usually unable to sustain an independent way of life— or self-esteem.

Left: Five Plains children, dressed in uncomfortable clothing, pose awkwardly for their picture in this 1898 reservation scene.

assumed that native Americans would adapt willingly if they were educated about the material and cultural benefits offered.

By the 1930s, the world of his ancestors seemed irretrievably lost to the Oglala Sioux holy man Black Elk, who had lived through war, Catholic missionizing, and reorganiza-

tion. In his autobiography *Black Elk Speaks* (recorded in 1930 through interviews with poet John Neihardt), he lamented:

I am sending a voice, Great Spirit, my Grandfather, forgetting nothing you have made, the stars of the universe and the grasses of the earth.…Today I send a voice for a people in despair.…Again, and maybe the last time on this earth, I recall the great vision you sent me. It may be that some little root of the sacred tree still lives. Nourish it then, that it may leaf and bloom and fill with singing birds. Hear me, not for myself, but for my people; I am old. Hear me that they may once more go back into the sacred hoop and find the good red road, the shielding tree!…Hear me in my sorrow, for I may never call again. O make my people live!

Later, Black Elk would detail the Sioux religion for anthropologist Joseph E. Brown in *The Sacred Pipe* (1953). The faith and tenacity of Black Elk—and elders of many other tribes—helped to preserve spiritual traditions as they were driven underground, but not extinguished, by U.S. legislation banning native religious practice.

Carlos Montezuma (Wassaja) lived through the transitional times of Black Elk, but his experiences were quite different. He was adopted by a Baptist minister several years after his childhood separation from his Yavapai Apache parents. After living with the fruits of "civilization"—including a university education and years of practice as a medical doctor—the process of assimilation had not prevented his becoming a radical and influential spokesman for native rights. He believed that the Bureau of Indian Affairs was patronizing and wrong-headed in its approach and he campaigned for its abolition. The B.I.A.'s guiding policy, "that the Indian must be cared for like a little child," as he put it, directly encouraged dependency and a loss of self-determination that doomed the reservations to failure on any terms, he argued. As an attempt to remove native cultures and superimpose another set of values on those who had survived the fight for land, the reservations would, indeed, fail.

Legislation in Canada

With the addition of British Columbia in 1871, the Dominion of Canada stretched from the Atlantic to the Pacific, but legal title to much of the country remained in native or Métis hands. From the late nineteenth to the mid-twentieth century, politicians in Ottawa were content to leave the territory they regarded as barely habitable under native control, but they did attempt to assimilate those tribes whose land was now contested ground.

In 1876 the Canadian Parliament passed the Indian Act, which defined federal adminis-tration of the native population and their lands. As in the United States, protection against further land encroachment was offered through strong managerial control of the Indian reserves, effected by an enforced system of local "band councils." Hereditary and consensually chosen chiefs were deposed,

and matrilineality—tracing descent and thus tribal identity through the female line—was officially abolished. The purpose of the band councils in Canada (and the tribal councils in the U.S.) was not to grant native people the limited degree of self-government that was enshrined in the legislation, but to ensure that government orders were carried out. The 1876 act included a policy of "enfranchise-ment," the right to vote in federal elections, for those who would give up membership in their own nations forever. Not many took up this offer.

The Indian Affairs Department began to implement the Indian Act by overthrowing traditional governments in the Iroquois terri-tories of Ontario and Quebec. In response, the Mohawks of the Bay of Quinte on Lake Ontario sent a plea to the governor general, Queen Victoria's representative in Canada:

Above: *Change was slow to affect this isolated Canadian Rockies community.*

Opposite: *The photographer of this early twentieth-century scene on a Blackfeet reservation termed it "their first Thanksgiving," though buffalo might have been a more welcome feast.*

> *"What is your power and authority to rule our people?"*
>
> —MOHAWK SPOKESMAN, 1877

Above: *Preparing pemmican, this Tsuu T'ina woman of Alberta employs traditional methods of drying the meat.*

We do not want our Council Fire extinguished, because it was the custom and manner of our forefathers.... We will remind you of the covenant Chain of Peace and Friendship between the English people and the Six Nations.... At the time of formation of the treaties...the Six Nations Indians were found and looked upon as a people, and had a systematic constitution.... It was understood by both parties...that each should maintain their own constitutions, but in the present instance, it appears that the Silver Chain is now tarnished upon these points.

The Canadian Government, which does not recognize us fully, looks upon the Six Nations as minors and treats them as such.... What is your power and authority to rule our people?

The question of the legitimacy of the government's authority was not addressed; the band councils were recognized by the government to the exclusion of any other representation. The rents, annuities, and other funds due the Mohawks by treaty would be dispersed only through the band council.

An example of the painful transitions to the new style of government occurred at the Mohawk territory of Akwesasne, which spanned the U.S.-Canadian border. In 1898 the clan mothers of Akwesasne wrote a long letter of protest to the governor general. In response, in 1899, mounted police were sent to enforce the installation of the authorized band council. According to the account of Michael Mitchell, an Akwesasne chief, the police summoned the chiefs to a meeting, and: "As the chiefs walked into the council office, they were thrown to the floor and handcuffed. One of the women notified the Head Chief, Jake Fire, and as he came through the door demanding the release of his fellow chiefs he was shot twice, the second shot being fatal. The police marched their prisoners to the tugboat and left the village." A Quebec newspaper, the *Huntingdon Gleaner,* commented on the incident:

The whites have been the aggressors all through the wretched affair, which has had so tragic an ending. It was the whites who passed a law to interfere with the internal management of an inoffensive tribe.... The Indians were merely resisting change to the customs that are dear to them, and which concern themselves alone.... They simply ask to be let alone, an independent community, ruled by themselves, and we do not see why what they ask should be withheld.

Protest notwithstanding, the policy was enforced over the next decades. Duncan Campbell Scott stated in 1920, when he was Canada's head of Indian affairs, that "Our object is to continue until there is not a single Indian

"To punish us for trying to preserve our rights, the Canadian Government has now pretended to abolish our government."

—DESKAHEH, 1925

in Canada that has not been absorbed." By this time, only Grand River (Ontario) was left of the original independent Iroquois councils.

Unheard by authorities in Canada, Deskaheh, a Cayuga Seneca leader, took a sovereignty protest on behalf of the Grand River council to Britain and the League of Nations, to no avail. In October 1924 armed Canadian police seized documents and sacred artifacts at Grand River and finally enforced the dissolution of the Six Nations parliament. In 1925 the exiled Deskaheh said:

Left: An Inuit child, oblivious to the changes affecting her nation, snuggles her best friend.

Above: *The expressions of this family on a reservation in Banff give little away.*

My home is on the Grand River… where, one hundred and forty winters ago, we had a little seashore of our own and a birch-bark navy.…To punish us for trying to preserve our rights, the Canadian Government has now pretended to abolish our government [and] set up a Canadian-made government over us, composed of the few traitors among us who are willing to accept pay from Ottawa.…If, one hundred and sixty-six winters ago, our warriors had not helped the British at Quebec…it would have been a French-speaking people here today, not you. That part of your history cannot be blotted out by the stealing of our wampum belts in which that is recorded.

Deskaheh's sentiments on the legitimacy of government rule would be echoed throughout the twentieth century.

The U.S. Allotment Experience

One of the most drastic pieces of legislation affecting native people in the United States came in the form of the 1887 Allotment Act, so called because it divided tribal lands into individual units for use by individual families. Before allotment, tribes had been free to organize the use and division of land in their reser-

vations. Those with an agricultural tradition, such as the Cherokee, Seminole, and Creek, did very well. Those like the Sioux who had been hunters were more resistant to the changes, yet they too managed to adapt.

The Allotment Act was also known as the Dawes Act, after its sponsor, Senator Henry Dawes of Massachusetts. Dawes had become an "expert" on the subject of native lands through his brief tour of the Cherokee Nation's new residence (in modern Oklahoma). Upon his return to Washington, D.C., the senator commented:

There is not a pauper in that nation, and the nation does not owe a dollar. It built its own capitol,…its schools and hospitals. Yet the defect of the system was apparent. They have got as far as they can go, because they hold their land in common.…There is no selfishness, which is at the bottom of civilization.

The Dawes Act authorized the president to partition reservations and assign parcels to individuals: 160 acres to each head of a family, lesser amounts to single adults, minors, and orphans. The fact that 160 acres of prime agricultural land differed vastly from 160 acres of desert was overlooked; where many families failed to make a success of their allotted land, this was often a simple function of its unproductive nature.

Excess reservation land after allotment could be purchased by the government with tribal consent, the proceeds being held in the U.S. Treasury for use by tribal members for "education and civilization." Allotment thus effectively opened up millions of acres for inexpensive purchase by non-native farmers. This 1914 Utah advertisement for land belonging to the Utes was one example among many:

Are you interested in the purchase, on easy terms, of a tract of land on which to build for yourself a home, obtaining with such purchase and without cost the privilege of occupying and cultivating adjoining lands? These lands are fertile. The climate is excellent. The lands are virgin. Canals are in place. Water covered by Primary Filings is abundant. There will be no taxes and no water assessments except on the purchased tract and, on that, only when the final payment has been made.

Thousands responded. The Utes watched the newcomers lay claim to the best lands on their reservation.

"[Allotment is] a mighty pulverizing engine to break up the tribal mass."

—THEODORE ROOSEVELT

Many viewed allotment as a terrible threat to tribal life. Ely Parker, who had been President Grant's Commissioner of Indian Affairs, favored assimilation but hated allotment: "The Indians as a body are deadly opposed to the scheme, for they see too plainly the certain and speedy dissolution of their tribal and national organizations." President Theodore Roosevelt, on the other hand, praised allotment as "a mighty pulverizing engine to break up the tribal mass." An Oklahoma Creek summed up the native opposition with the comment: "Egypt had its locusts,…England its black plague. But it was left for the unfortunate Indian Territory to be afflicted with the worst scourge of the nineteenth century, the Dawes Commission."

Under the Dawes Act, native Americans on allotted land received U.S. citizenship—citizenship for all native Americans would not be granted until 1924. The act specified:

Every Indian born within the territorial limits of the United States who has voluntarily taken up…his residence separate and apart from any tribe of Indians therein, and has adopted the habits of civilized life, is hereby declared to be a citizen of the United States, and is entitled to all the rights, privileges, and immunities of such citizens, whether said Indian has been or not, by birth or otherwise, a member of any tribe of Indians

within the territorial limits of the United States without in any manner impairing or otherwise affecting the right of any such Indian to tribal or other property.

Section 8 of the act stipulated its territorial scope. Its provisions did not extend to the territory occupied by the Cherokees, Creeks, Choctaws, Chickasaws, and Seminoles (in modern Oklahoma); nor to the Seneca Nation in the state of New York; nor to a Sioux-occupied strip of territory in the state of Nebraska, among other exceptions. The act exempted a dozen tribes for a variety of reasons, including stipulations in previous treaties. Some, including the Navajo and Apache in the Southwest, were exempt primarily because their lands were considered worthless for cultivation. These exceptions did not prevent further pioneer encroachment onto native lands in the years following the passage of the act. In 1890 the United States annexed the western half of the Indian Territory, renaming it "The Territory of Oklahoma," and in 1893, more than 10,000 square miles of Cherokee prairie was declared open. Settlers rushed to stake their claims.

Following pages: *(Left) Women carrying their heavy burdens of water supplied by a government well in Araibi, Arizona. (Right) Successive governments believed that assimilation was the most efficient solution to the "Indian problem." Agents thought that handing out clothing was the first step toward making their youngest charges "regular kids."*

Below: *A Blackfeet reservation still life, with hand-laced tipi, family members and animals, and an unexpected addition— the sewing machine.*

123

When the Cherokee Nation and more than a dozen other tribes fought the Dawes Act in court, Congress replied by passing the Curtis Act of 1898, which dissolved the governments that had been established within the Five Civilized Tribes (Cherokees, Chickasaws, Creeks, Choctaws, and Seminoles). A substance had just been found under the lands of the Civilized Tribes that was just as dangerous to Indians as gold: oil.

Within those tribes most affected by the Dawes Act, there was resistance. Frank Fools Crow, a spiritual elder of the Oglala Sioux on the Pine Ridge Reservation in South Dakota, provided one such voice. Under the new system, he said:

The Cherokee Strip

September 16, 1893, brought the largest-ever opening of Indian lands in the West to settlement. The Cherokee Strip, or Outlet, in north-central Oklahoma, and the Tonkawa and Pawnee reservations—a total of some 6,500,000 acres—were opened to homesteaders. In buckboards, on horseback, in covered wagons, even on foot, some 50,000 people rushed into the area to stake their claims. Technically, the money obtained from these sales belonged to the Indians, but its disbursement was in the hands of the Bureau of Indian Affairs. Only a month before, the Osage had prudently refused to sell their 2,000,000 acres in Oklahoma, adjacent to the Cherokee Strip, to the federal government. However, they would not be exempt from the widespread friction that had been increasing since the creation of the Oklahoma Territory in 1890.

Right: *Eight Crow prisoners who fell foul of Montana authorities in 1887. The Crow were known as a remarkably vigorous and independent people.*

Opposite: *A Tesuque Pueblo woman renews the mud coating on the adobe walls of her dwelling.*

[We] would have to separate and live as families on our own land. We all knew it would not be easy to be tied down and dependent...for the things we needed to live....The buffalo were all gone....It was especially hard to have the children sent away to school, and that was resisted, as was the order to cut our hair short. People were also unhappy about relatives being moved to reservations some distance away. And we were also not pleased about the interference in our religious ceremonies.

The Dawes Act stipulated that title to each allotted land parcel would be held by the federal government for twenty-five years to prevent its sale. In 1891 the act was amended to allow leasing of allotted land. The effect of this was to undermine the protection of the twenty-five-year clause, and when its consequences became apparent, opposition to leasing grew quickly. Wealthy cattle ranchers and homesteaders alike rushed to take advantage of the opportunity to occupy newly opened land, to the detriment of reservation economies. On an Assiniboine reservation, "They leased our reservation to a big cattle company. In one year after that we were flat broke." Frank Fools Crow wrote of the effect of leasing at Pine Ridge:

[The locals] encouraged the destitute Oglalas to sell or to lease their allotments to them and then to move into towns....So people left their once fine log homes and storage cellars and settled down in tents and shacks. They exchanged their freedom for money and liquor, and as it turned out there would be no end of this curse.

"They exchanged their freedom for money and liquor, and as it turned out there would be no end of this curse."

—FRANK FOOLS CROW

Women's Work

Much native history is written in the artefacts of women, inspired by and made of materials from nature. These artefacts vary widely across culture areas, but there are commonalities. In many traditions, women fashioned containers for gathering and transport: baskets, pouches, and bags made from animal hide or woven of reeds, grasses, bark, and buffalo or mountain-goat hair. These objects bore tribal symbols ranging from lightning bolts to bear claws and thunderbirds.

Women were often responsible for constructing the family dwelling, whether permanent, like the Southwestern adobe cliff houses, or temporary, like the tipis that accompanied the Plains Indians on their pursuit of the buffalo. The Tesuque Pueblo woman at right is shown maintaining the adobe walls of her home. Many skills were involved in making a *wickiup* of reeds or brush, or fleshing and tanning hides sewn together to cover pole frameworks. These activities were often accompanied by traditional prayers and songs, as were the fashioning of tools and ceremonial objects.

In some tribes, women learn traditional skills as potters, producing a wide range of earthenware vessels for carrying water, cooking, food preparation, and storage. These skills have been passed from mother to daughter, along with local knowledge for making clothing for everyday and ceremonial use. Such clothing often denoted the wearer's tribal affiliation and status, with quillwork done in dyed porcupine quills, or beadwork, or painted designs.

In addition to these skills, women have acquired and passed down specialized agricultural knowledge and routinely performed tasks requiring tremendous stamina and physical strength. Their artefacts, homes, and cultivation techniques are testament to their vital role in traditional economies.

Native American women have also been keepers of native culture and activists, as demonstrated in the efforts of Paiute spokeswoman and author Sarah Winnemucca.

Above: *Omaha boys photographed at the Carlisle Indian School, Pennsylvania, in 1880. The schoolchildren's individuality was undermined; their heritage was erased in an effort to enforce the mores of the dominant culture. Some were able to benefit from the rigorous education. Others were simply miserable.*

But worse was to come than the leasing amendment, in the form of the 1906 Burke Act, which allowed the secretary of the interior to transfer title of land whenever he deemed that "any Indian allottee is competent and capable of managing his or her affairs." When volunteers to take title to — and sell — their land dwindled, the Indian Bureau conducted home-to-home solicitations on many reservations to persuade allottees to accept their titles. In 1917 the very right to refuse was removed from anyone of at least half white ancestry, now deemed competent and issued title automatically with immediate effect. Those who had attended government schools were pronounced competent after brief interviews. By 1920 more than half the native population living on designated allotment land under the Dawes Act were formally without land, and a large proportion of the remaining land was leased to non-native occupants.

From the Washington, D.C., perspective, the policies of reservation allotment and assimilation were successful in opening land to western settlers and ranchers, but there was still an "Indian problem." In 1926 the U.S. secretary of the interior commissioned a comprehensive study of native affairs by the Institute for Government Research, a privately endowed organization. The study's conclusions, known as the Meriam Report, issued in 1928, amounted to an 850-page denouncement of government policy: nearly half the native population lived on a per capita income of less than $200 per year (the U.S. average was $1,350); illiteracy was as high as 67 percent; health standards were poor — the tuberculosis mortality rate was seventeen times the national average. Allotment was a dismal failure. Native Americans were neither successfully assimilated nor able to live according to their traditions. Since the passage of the Dawes Act, native-owned land had been reduced to one third of the 1887 acreage.

The allotment and leasing "curse" would, indeed, have a long-term effect. In her autobiography, Mary Crow Dog, Lakota Sioux, described economic conditions on the Rosebud Reservation during her childhood in the 1950s: "We were not taught any skills [at school]. The land was leased to white ranchers. Jobs were almost nonexistent on the reservation, and outside the res whites did not hire Indians if they could help it."

An Inexorable Erosion of Cultures

By the early twentieth century, reservation-based native Americans were no longer widely viewed as posing the powerful and dangerous threat the westward migrants had feared during the expansionist period. Historian E. Benjamin Andrews expressed in his *History of the United States* (1906) an attitude shared by many whites:

Of arts, the red man had but the rudest. He made wigwams, canoes, bone fish-hooks with lines of hide or twisted bark, stone tomahawks, arrow-heads and spears, clothing of skins, wooden bows, arrows, and clubs. He loved fighting, finery, gambling and the chase. He domesticated no animals but the dog and possibly the hog. Sometimes brave, he was oftener treacherous, cruel, revengeful.

Some displayed a curiosity, even respect, for these "rude" people and their ways, but even as such interest developed, government officials were undermining native American cultures as quickly and steadily as they could. Ritual and ceremonial expressions of tradi-

"Our annals…were stored in our song and dance rituals, our history…was not stored in books, but in the living memory."

—Luther Standing Bear

tional faiths were banned, because the government saw them as endangering the process of assimilation and stirring up potential resistance. The primary method for replacing native values with the "white" way across North America was through education. Children were taken from their families and enrolled in boarding schools, where they would be stripped of their given names and forced to speak only in English. Brought up in an oral tradition, they were thrust into a linear culture, as pointed out by Luther Standing Bear,

Oglala Sioux, who attended the Carlisle School in Pennsylvania: "Our annals, all happenings of human import, were stored in our song and dance rituals, our history differing in that it was not stored in books, but in the living memory. So, while the white people had much to teach us, we had much to teach them, and what a school could have been established upon that idea!"

The schools were located far from the reservations in an attempt (not always successful) to prevent runaways. At most schools, the chil-

Below: Studying math at the Carlisle School, 1900.

dren were not well cared for. Epidemics created by overcrowding and poor nutrition resulted in unusually high mortality rates. The shock of leaving a loving home for an institution was devastating, and the emotional scars that resulted were passed on to the next generation. One Navajo mother wept: "When we put our children in school, it is like giving our hearts up."

In spite of the risk, some native leaders, including Geronimo, the Chiricahua Apache leader and medicine man, ordered their young kinsmen and successors to attend such schools. As Geronimo's nephew explained: "Without this training in the ways of the White Eyes, our people could never compete with them. So it was necessary that those destined for leadership prepare themselves to cope with the enemy."

Oglala Sioux chief Frank Fools Crow did not attend a boarding school, but he gave a clear exposition of his thoughts on the new versus the old ways of life:

In the period from 1895 to 1910, we Sioux learned a great deal about our new home life, family life, and social life. Some of our young people kept wishing we could return to the old ways, but our elders made it plain that it would not happen. They said the new way was here to stay, and the Sioux had no choice but to learn it.... From what I have been told, our old life-way was constantly assaulted by white pressures from the middle of the nineteenth century until the Custer affair in 1876.

I would choose the prewhite days for two reasons: There was no liquor then, and it would be pleasant to live without the havoc that has worked among us. Also, in the ancient days our religious life was respected and powerful.

As a ten-year-old boy, Luther Standing Bear, a descendant of chiefs, agreed to leave the Pine Ridge Reservation to attend the government's Carlisle Boarding School in Pennsylvania. As he recalled much later,

I could think of no reason why white people wanted Indian boys and girls except to kill them, and not having the remotest idea of

what a school was, I thought we were going East to die....It was only about three years after the Custer battle, and the general opinion was that the Plains people merely infested the earth as nuisances, and our being there simply evidenced misjudgment on the part of Wakan Tanka [God]. Whenever our train stopped at the railway stations, it was met by great numbers of white people who came to gaze upon the little Indian "savages."...On the train the older boys sang brave songs in an effort to keep up their spirits and ours too.

At the school, the young people had their hair cut off and were issued uncomfortable uniforms in place of their traditional clothing. Their names were changed to common English names, and their normal diet was replaced by white

bread, coffee, sugar, and other unwholesome food to which they were unaccustomed. Lack of exercise contributed to ill health. As Luther Standing Bear recalled it: "The change in clothing, housing, food, and confinement combined with lonesomeness was too much, and in three years, nearly one half of the children from the Plains were dead and through with all earthly schools. In the graveyard at Carlisle, most of the graves are those of little ones."

Similar off-reservation schools were set up in Indian Territory, New Mexico, Arizona, and California. Half the children's time was spent in the classroom, the other half in learning vocational and industrial skills like dairy farming and printing. The use of Indian languages was punished, and visits home were so infrequent that some children returned to the reservations

Opposite, above: *At the Phoenix Indian School in Arizona, one child finds the camera more interesting than praying.*

Opposite, below: *A young educator at a progressive school teaches a group of Navajo children English as well as a phonetic script for their own language.*

Above: *Reading, writing, and arithmetic at a makeshift trailer school on a Navajo reservation.*

Right: *Sarah Winnemucca, Paiute activist, diplomat, and writer.*

to find that relatives had died in their absence.

On the positive side, the children forged close ties with one another at the schools, which would lead to intermarriage and other forms of multitribal relationships as they grew up. Some became activists on behalf of their people and took part in pan-Indian political groups.

> *"I would place all the Indians of Nevada [in] New York…as immigrants, that they might be received with open arms, blessed with universal suffrage."*
>
> —SARAH WINNEMUCCA

One such activist was Sarah Winnemucca, a Paviotso Paiute of northern Nevada. Her given name was Tocmetone, or Shell Flower. She encountered racism as an adolescent attending Catholic school in California's San Joaquin Valley and was orphaned after the Paiute War of 1860.

Below: *Boys will be Boy Scouts: these Yaqui children are supervised as they build their own clubhouse from adobe bricks.*

Using her language skills to good effect, she dealt with unscrupulous Indian agents and sought to make peace between the government and an allied Paiute-Bannock force in 1878. Finally, she took to the East Coast lecture circuit to publicize the difficulties faced by her people. At times her frustration at the lack of response was evident, as expressed in one of her lectures:

> *If I possessed the wealth…I would place all the Indians of Nevada on ships in our harbor, take them to New York and land them there as immigrants, that they might be received with open arms, blessed with universal suffrage…out of the reach of Indian agents.*

In 1883 she published the autobiographical *Life Among the Piutes* (the tribe name was spelled "Piute" at that time). Despite her tireless efforts, her personal life suffered when promises that had been made during negotiations on behalf of her tribe failed to materialize, and she was blamed by many for the broken faith. She died of tuberculosis in 1891 before she was fifty years old.

On Display: From Anthropology to Wild West Shows

The strictures against Indian ceremonials that had been outlined in the 1883 *Code of Religious Offences* were not completely successful. Plains Tribes like the Kiowa, Comanche, and Ponca transferred their summer Sun Dances to secret locations. Some tribes built windowless roundhouses to conceal their activities from Indian agents and their spies. Others carried out their traditional ceremonies under the pretext of celebrating Independence Day or another "acceptable" holiday.

Early in the twentieth century, native Americans found unexpected allies among anthropologists and others concerned about preserving their culture and lifeways. The Bureau of American Ethnology, created in 1879, sent out field workers like Alice Fletcher and James Mooney to learn all they could about the "vanishing" Indian, who had gained new status as a romantic symbol of the nation's past. Anthropologist Franz Boas published his *Handbook of American Indian Languages* (the basis for his later four-volume treatise of the same name) in 1911. John Wesley Powell's seminal work, *Introduction to the Study of Indian Languages*, had appeared a few decades earlier. Boas understood that Indian languages were key to understanding the cultures of the hundreds of different tribes that were facing extinction. "A student of Mohammedan life in Arabia or Turkey," he reasoned, "would hardly be considered a serious investigator if all his knowledge had to be derived from second-hand accounts. The ethnologist, on the other hand, undertakes in the majority of cases to elucidate the innermost thoughts and feelings of a people without so much as a smattering of knowledge of their language."

Right: *The excavation of this ancient housing complex at Pueblo Grande, a "lost city" in Nevada, was undertaken in the 1920s by a team of Zuni workers and Dr. M.R. Harrington of the Museum of the American Indian's Heye Foundation.*

Opposite: *By the mid-1920s the sheer volume of the holdings of New York's Museum of the American Indian had become so great that an annex was built in the Bronx. Here, two men prepare to move Kwakiutl totem poles from the main museum to the new building.*

John Wesley Powell was the first curator of the Smithsonian Institution's Bureau of American Ethnology and an inspiration to other anthropologists like John Bourke. While historians including Frederick Jackson Turner saw westward expansion as a source of American strength, more thoughtful ethnologists like John Bourke focused on the greed that powered the drive on the frontier and its scandalous treatment of native cultures.

Bourke was one of many early investigators who had spent time in the army fighting Indians, and who thereby became interested in their lives. Unlike armchair theorists back East, men like Bourke and Lt. James H. Bradley observed native Americans firsthand, went to live with them, and became accepted and appreciated by them to some degree. Bourke became a staunch supporter of Indian rights. In a letter to his friend Herbert Welsh (1894) about the eight-year imprisonment of the Chiricahuas, he said:

It did not take me long to see that all the War Department wanted was quiet; [it] did not intend to do anything at all for the Chiricahuas, but it would avoid as much as possible any popular clamor.... The only way to get anything out of these practical politicians is to fire hot shot and shell at them.

Amateur archaeologist Richard Wetherill was a rancher near Mesa Verde, Colorado, during the late 1800s. He and his brothers became friendly with Indians living near them. Wetherill wondered what he might find in Cliff Canyon, one of the deepest and most impenetrable in Mesa Verde. Acowitz, a Ute friend, told him that the ancient ones had lived deep in that canyon, near its head, in a place no white man knew of. He warned Wetherill against seeking out the lost city, for fear of disturbing the spirits of the dead.

In 1888 Wetherill and his brothers were hunting for stray cattle when they first saw what he

> *"The only way to get anything out of these practical politicians is to fire hot shot and shell at them."*
>
> —JOHN BOURKE, 1894

would call the Cliff Palace at Mesa Verde—a 400-room dwelling high in the canyon wall. It looked as though the inhabitants had abandoned the place in a hurry. Earthen bowls, mugs, and water jars had been set down as though their owners might return at any moment. The Wetherills also found skeletons.

Excavating carefully, using what tools they had, they began to retrieve the objects and skeletons from the cave. Later, archaeologists would fault them for using inadequate methods, but the brothers worked conscientiously, taking pictures and making notes. In the spring of 1892, their collection was bought by C.D. Hazard of the H. Jay Smith Exploring Co. for exhibition the following year at the World's Columbian Exposition at Chicago. Eventually, all of the specimens—more than a thousand skeletons, pottery shards, weapons, and baskets—found their way to museums. Partly as a result of the Chicago exhibition, the American Museum of Natural History in New York was reorganized, and German-born Franz Boas, one of the pioneers of anthropology, became its curator in 1901.

In their zeal to study North America's many tribes, anthropologists and others dug up native American bones by the hundreds of thousands. Most of them ended up stored in cartons and boxes in museums across the country, awaiting the day when activists would demand their return for proper burial or other funeral rites.

While the views and actions of early social scientists seem grossly insensitive from the modern perspective, most U.S. citizens of the era derived their beliefs about native Americans from sources like exposition sideshows and the Wild West Shows. No longer a threat, Indians were now widely perceived as a curiosity and a symbol of times past. The myth of the American West was embodied in the Wild West Show beginning in 1876, when Buffalo Bill's famous show began playing to packed houses in California. William F. Cody had been a scout for the army and an Indian fighter. He had come to understand native Americans and something of their cultures by spending time with them—earning their respect in return. He also had a strong flair for showmanship.

By 1886 Cody's show was in demand not only on the East Coast, but overseas. When it came

Mythmakers: Remington And Russell

Two important American artists responded
to the call of the frontier West and became
famous as painters and sculptors of the Plains
Indians, cowboys, soldiers, and animals of the
region. Frederic Remington (1861–1909) studied at Yale University and in New York City
before traveling west for his health. He worked
as a cowboy and lived for some time among
Plains Indian tribes. He painted realistic and
colorful pictures, including *The Smoke Signal*
(illustrated), *A Dash for the Timber*, and *The
Last Stand*. He also made action-filled bronze
sculptures like the famous Bronco Buster, and

wrote and illustrated five books, including *The
Way of an Indian*.

His contemporary Charles M. Russell (1865–
1926) was another self-taught artist born during the Civil War era. He left his native St.
Louis, Missouri, at the age of sixteen to become
a cowboy in Montana, where he remained for
the rest of his life. His most popular works
include the sculpture *When the Sioux and
Blackfeet Meet*, depicting a pitched battle on
the Plains, and the paintings *Waiting for a
Chinook* and *Lewis and Clark at Ross' Hole* (for
the Montana House of Representatives).

Ishi: The Last of His Tribe

In August 1911 the last member of the Yahi Yana tribe, native to the northern Sacramento Valley, was discovered in Oroville, California. He had never come into contact with a non-native and was unable to communicate verbally, so he was nicknamed Ishi—the Yahi Yana word for man. Two anthropologists from the University of California, Alfred L. Kroeber and T.T. Waterman, were given custody of this living "relic" and brought Ishi to the university's museum of anthropology. He expected to be executed there, since his tribe had been reduced from some 2,000 members to a handful of survivors by marauding whites. The survivors had taken refuge in the hills, where their numbers dwindled until only Ishi and his mother were left. When she died, he left the hills and walked south to the point where he was found crouched in a corral. Visitors flocked to the university to see the man who soon became known as the "last wild Indian." There Ishi demonstrated tasks typical of the Yahi Yana people—making fire and shaping stone arrowheads and spear points—to the visitors. In 1916, only five years after he was discovered, Ishi died, and another native American tribe was irrevocably lost.

to New York, celebrities like William Tecumseh Sherman, Mark Twain, and General Custer's widow came to see it. It was Twain who inspired Cody to take the show abroad; he was impressed by what he perceived as the authenticity of the show, and in 1886 he wrote to Cody:

Down to its smallest details the Show is genuine. It brought back vividly the breezy wild life of the Plains and the Rocky Mountains. It is wholly free from sham and insincerity and the effects it produced upon me by its spectacles were identical with those wrought upon me a long time ago on the frontier.

Several already-famous native Americans were engaged by Cody's traveling troupe, including Sitting Bull and Black Elk of the Hunkpapa and Oglala Sioux, respectively. In 1885 Sitting Bull signed a four-month contract that would pay him $50 a week, a bonus of $125, and exclusive rights to the sale of his portraits and autographs, of which there were many. General Sherman commented bitterly: "Sitting Bull is a humbug but has a popular fame on which he has a natural right to 'bank.'"

On the road, Sitting Bull made friends with Annie Oakley, whom he admired and made his adopted daughter. Cody attempted to present him in a dignified manner, not like a figure in a wax museum. He enjoyed personal freedom, rode in parades, and greeted visitors at his tipi. He also lavished his earnings on his family and friends in need, rather than saving money for himself.

"The love of possession is a disease with them."

—SITTING BULL

After touring Europe with Buffalo Bill in the 1880s, Sitting Bull observed to Annie Oakley, "The white man knows how to make everything, but he does not know how to distribute it.... The love of possession is a disease with them. They take tithes from the poor and weak to support the rich who rule. They claim this

mother of ours, the earth, for their own and fence their neighbors away."

Black Elk, who was to become a holy man of his people, joined the Cody show as a boy of twenty-two and toured all over England. Queen Victoria was impressed by her meeting with the Indians of Cody's troupe, but expressed her regret that they were being "exhibited" like animals in a menagerie. "America is a good country," Black Elk recalled her saying, "and I have seen all kinds of people, but today I have seen the best looking people—the Indians. I am very glad to see them." Black Elk and four other men gave a private show for the queen at which they performed the Omaha Grass Dance.

Despite their drawbacks, both the Indian boarding schools and the Wild West Show served as a means for members of tribes from different parts of the country to get to know each other. These friendships and the solidarity they engendered would prove important to pan-Indian efforts on behalf of civil rights during the twentieth century.

Merchants began to take a greater interest in Indian artwork and design as wider exposure created a demand for it. Along with the 1893 Chicago Exposition and the Wild West Show came Fred Harvey, whose restaurant and hotel enterprises, which he had established along the route of the Santa Fe Railroad from the 1870s, also generated exposure to, and interest in, native arts and crafts. In partnership with the railway, Harvey's company contributed to the rise of Southwest tourism. Advertising, picture postcards, fair displays, and sales facilities encouraged middle-class Americans to acknowledge and acquaint themselves with the native cultures of New Mexico and Arizona. Fred Harvey died in 1901, but the company's Indian Department, established by his daughter Minnie in 1902, evolved as a new enterprise. The Indian Department collected and dealt in traditional art through traders like J.L. Hubbell of Ganado, Arizona. It also worked with dealers, scholars, and major institutions like the American Museum of Natural History in New York and the Carnegie Museum in Pittsburgh.

Above: *Tourists visiting a pueblo in Santo Domingo, New Mexico.*

Opposite: *After years of negotiation, the Gros Ventre of North Dakota recovered their rain-making talisman—two human skulls wrapped in a sacred bundle—from Dr. George C. Heye, head of the Museum of the American Indian.*

Right: *Buffalo Bill's Wild West Show helped make "cowboys and Indians" a popular form of entertainment.*

Architect Mary Elizabeth Jane Colter had been hired by Fred Harvey to design many of the railroad-related facilities that he built across the West. Inspired by Richard Wetherill's Mesa Verde collection at the Chicago exposition, she used Southwestern motifs, local building styles and materials, and native artists to realize her designs at the Grand Canyon and other notable hotels and terminals. The American Arts and Crafts movement found much to admire in native pottery, jewelry, basketry, and other arts and skills. However, native opinions on such enterprises were mixed. Many of the "artworks" in demand were sacred ritual objects, like the Hopi kachina dolls, never meant to be seen outside the Pueblo cultures, much less sold as trinkets or toys. In other cases, like that of Pueblo potter Maria Martinez and her family, who took part in Harvey's Painted Desert Exhibit at the Panama-California Exposition of 1915, new prosperity accrued to the community with the renaissance of traditional skills.

Above: *A Hopi kachina—a sacred object, not a toy.*

Right: *As part of the celebration of electrification of the Illinois Central Railroad, a pageant showed an entertaining version of the perils of travelers past.*

> *"I asked the woman how long it took her to make the rug, and she told me six months. The trader told her he would pay her $140 for it in trade."*
>
> —SAM AHKEAH

During the reservation era, the trading post continued to provide a source of income for native Americans. Until the 1960s, however, the terms of exchange were highly unfavorable, as described by Navajo chief Sam Ahkeah in an interview conducted during the 1950s:

We depend on our lamb and wool money every year. Our other money comes from the jewelry made by the men and rugs made by the women.... Our people make very little money doing these things. I stopped by the house of one of my people a few days ago, and

Below: Movie Night at Taos Theater, *a 1939 oil painting by Oscar E. Berninghaus.*

Above: *Trading posts facilitated sales to tourists on reservations—a source of income from traditional skills and a mixed blessing.*

the man wanted me to take his wife to the store to deliver a rug and buy supplies. I asked the woman how long it took her to make the rug, and she told me six months. The trader told her he would pay her $140 for it in trade. The family owed the store account $80. He gave her scrip for the balance....I expect the trader makes 200 percent profit.

Lakota chief Frank Fools Crow described another demoralizing program set up by the Bureau of Indian Affairs during the 1920s. Each person on the reservation was to receive a certain income with which to purchase supplies and clothing. This method was intended to replace the rationing systems, but the reservation residents did not have experience in managing their funds. And since they were not earning the money, their sense of empowerment and freedom was eroding steadily. Some even turned to theft when they got into financial trouble—in complete violation of Sioux tradition.

New Leadership and Support

Despite the bleak conditions on many reservations, and the ongoing struggle for land and water rights, the turn of the century brought some positive developments for the First Nations. Men and women who had resolved to see their people into a new chapter of their long history came forward as spokesmen and activists on behalf of Indian rights. They were joined by supporters like social worker John Collier, who came to Taos Pueblo, New Mexico,

Ethnicity in Vogue

Throughout the early 1900s, the white majority maintained an ambivalent attitude toward native Americans. This attitude was woven of diverse threads including guilt, superiority, curiosity, a perverse kind of national pride, and just plain ignorance. The result was often patronization that served no one well.

No longer seen as a territorial threat, native Americans were often a source of apparently benign amusement. Even the well-meaning were complacent in regarding Indians as "cute" or "quaint." Indian "princesses" in the idealized mode of Pocahontas were encouraged to compete in beauty contests (right) and lend ethnic romance to the proceedings. An archer and a dancer each offer a few pointers to their pupils (below)—in exchange for a photo opportunity.

These patronizing overtures did little to build an improved relationship between native Americans and the dominant culture. Well-intentioned as some may have been, the results were to further diminish pride in their suppressed cultural heritage.

*Right: The dreamcatcher—
protection from
night-time harm.*

*Opposite, above: Proving that
their spirit was not easily
quelled, two aged representatives of Kansas's Potowatomi
tribe met with Secretary of the
Interior Dr. Hubert Work in
1923 to press their claims to a
land grant on the shores of
Lake Michigan.*

*Opposite, below: California
members of the Indian Rights
Association lobby their state
representative for a
Congressional act on behalf of
their land rights in 1937.*

*Below: John Collier, social
worker and head of the Bureau
of Indian Affairs, with Chief
Paul Red Eagle and his wife.*

in 1920 and worked tirelessly to form the American Indian Defense Association, protecting Pueblo land rights.

Santee Sioux Charles Eastman attended Dartmouth College and earned an M.D. from Boston University in 1890. Working as a physician at the Pine Ridge Reservation, he was a witness to the grim aftermath of the Wounded Knee massacre, which changed his life. He moved back to his native Minnesota and began a career as a writer and social worker, during which he helped establish the Society of American Indians (SAI) in 1911. His people called him Ohiyesa—"Winner."

Another impressive advocate was Gertrude Simmons Bonnin, a Yankton Sioux born at Pine Ridge, who attended a Quaker boarding school in Wabash, Indiana. Later, she completed college and taught at

Carlisle Indian School before returning to South Dakota. Married in 1902 to Sioux tribesman Raymond T. Bonnin, she taught at Utah's Uintah and Ouray Reservation for ten years. She published stories of reservation life under the pen name Zitkala-Sa, "Red Bird." Her husband was one of some 17,000 native Americans who served in World War I with distinction. From 1916 Bonnin worked in Washington, D.C., as a champion of Indian rights. She was secretary of the SAI and founder of the National Council of American Indians.

Carlos Montezuma worked as a doctor on several reservations and also at the Carlisle Indian School. Outspoken in his criticism of reservation policy and the Indian Bureau, he told a Chicago audience in 1898 that the reservations were "a demoralized prison; a barrier against enlightenment, a promoter of idleness, beggary, gambling, pauperism, ruin, and death." Under his native name Wassaja, which means Signaling, he published a monthly magazine that advocated abolition of the Indian Bureau.

From the Northeast came Arthur Coswell Parker, born on New York's Cattaraugus Seneca Reservation in 1881 to a Seneca father and a white mother who taught school on the reservation. Raised partly in White Plains, New York, Parker pursued a career in anthropology, doing field work at his home reservation. He became a key member of the SAI and edited its journal, *The American Indian Magazine*, from 1911 to 1916.

Soon after the 1914 outbreak of World War I, hundreds of young native Americans crossed the border to sign up with Canadian units leaving for the European front. When the U.S. entered the conflict in 1917, another 10,000 native Americans saw active service in the U.S. Army, and 2,000 joined the Navy, while thousands more participated in Red Cross home programs, sewing over 100,000 items of clothing for troops overseas. Contributing to the war effort brought scant reward. Those who returned to the reservations had veterans' benefits, but had acquired new, worldly attitudes—including, all too often, harmful liquor habits. During their absence some reservations had been carved up under the land-leasing programs. "All we ask is full citizenship," commented Charles Eastman, summing up the resentment expressed by many. "Why not? We offered our services and our money in this war, and more in proportion to our number and means than any other race or class of the population."

> *"All we ask is full citizenship. We offered our services and our money in this war, and more in proportion to our number and means than any other race or class of the population."*
>
> —CHARLES EASTMAN, SANTEE SIOUX

In 1919 Congress finally granted citizenship to native American veterans of World War I, which opened the door to universal native American citizenship—a long-deferred goal that was not realized until 1924. The efforts of John Collier and other activists pressured the government for an Indian New Deal, which had its start in 1933 when President Franklin D. Roosevelt appointed Collier commissioner of Indian Affairs. The results were mixed. Collier's ambitious program became law as the Indian Reorganization Act in 1934. It reversed the controversial land allotment policy, which helped to ensure the integrity of tribal lands, and it

Right: *Chief Eagle Horse journeyed from subarctic Canada to New York City to urge volunteers to enlist for service in World War I.*

Below: *Returning veterans from both wars were not appreciated by all of those in whose name they had served.*

provided an apparently high degree of self-government in the formation of tribal corporations and executive bodies. A $10 million fund was established to promote economic enterprise, vocational training, and public schooling. Tribal languages, arts, and traditional skills were to be revived. Not all native Americans accepted the program, however. Oklahoma tribes, who had been without reservations since 1906, felt that the New Deal was "seeking to frustrate the opportunity of the Indian to enter American life as a citizen." Over a two-year period 181 of the tribes or bands that held referendums accepted the IRA, but 77 rejected it. Much benefit flowed to participating tribes—at least, in theory—in the form of business loans, jobs, education, housing, health care, and self-government that engendered new pride.

> *"It's not self-government because self-government by permission is no self-government at all."*
>
> —RAMON ROUBIDEAUX, SIOUX

The experience of those who accepted the IRA was, in practice, less than their expectations of the program. As under the Canadian Indian Act, the promises of new autonomy were somewhat illusory: "It's not self-government because self-government by permission is no self-government at all," said Ramon Roubideaux, a Sioux attorney. The economic climate of the Great Depression added to the problems created by earlier programs and made for hard times on the reservations, with or without the IRA. Writing in the 1950s, Ed Boyer, Shoshone-Bannock, condemned the entire deal:

The Indian Reorganization Act is a miserable failure. We were getting along much better here in this reservation [Fort Hall, Idaho] fifteen years ago than we are now. They told us that if we would vote to accept

"Special Powers"

Captivated by simplistic ideas about shamans, healing rites, and "nature worship," men and women dissatisfied with their Western spiritual heritage began to seek out native American "gurus" believed to have special powers of discernment. Once the Indians were safely immobilized on reservations, it became not only safe but, eventually, chic to attribute to them a wisdom that had been denigrated by earlier generations bent on conquest. Of course, many of those who sought to build bridges between native and Christian spirituality were motivated by genuine humility and a spirit of ecumenism. Too often, however, unsuspecting native Americans found themselves sought after as fonts of arcane knowledge, cast in the role of fortune tellers, "magical" healers, and mediators with the forces of nature. The result was more likely to be confusion than enlightenment for all concerned.

Above: *Faced with the options of remaining on reservations or joining the dominant culture, many natives, like these four Iroquois men, chose the latter.*

the provisions of the Indian Reorganization Act, everyone would have money to buy livestock and farming equipment, that we would have plenty of money in our pockets and be able to buy good automobiles too. As it turned out, it has helped only a few. Most of our people are in worse condition than they were before.

World War II brought reforms to an abrupt halt, as appropriations were reduced to nothing and large numbers of people were drafted. Native Americans served as pilots, navigators, and gunners in the air corps; machinists, spotters, and signalmen in the navy. Navajo code talkers helped the U.S. Marines throughout the war in the Pacific. War drums called members of the Osage tribe to repel the enemy only hours after the attack on Pearl Harbor. Hundreds of Osage men and women served in the armed forces, including Clarence L. Tinker, who became a major general in the Army Air Corps

before his death in combat. Other tribes with distinguished service records included the Hopi, Lakota, Sauk and Fox, Oneida, Ojibwa, and Comanche. Altogether, some 26,000 Indian men and women served. Some 46,000 others left tribal homelands to engage in wartime industrial work. For most, this was a first experience with mainstream urban life, throwing into relief both the benefits and the deficiencies of life on the reservation.

After the war, many of the old prejudices remained. State law still prevented native residents from voting in New Mexico and Arizona. Some returning native American veterans were denied G.I. loans. And Prohibition was still enforced on many reservations. There was widespread demand for an end to the existing trustee relationship between native Americans and the federal government. "Talk about German prison camps," said one Arapaho veteran, "we are prisoners of the Indian Bureau."

Relocated and Terminated

When the Cold War set in during the early 1950s, a "Fortress America" mentality encouraged the illusion of a happy, homogeneous country devoid of racial or cultural divisions. Collier's notion of preserving native American culture was a threat to this way of thinking. In 1945 the Bureau of Indian Affairs got a new commissioner: Dillon Myer, who had supervised the internment of Japanese-Americans during World War II. Myer saw urban integration as the solution to the "Indian Problem." With tribespeople off the land, reservations could be terminated and the government would be "out of the Indian business"—a popular slogan of the day.

The attack against tribal landholding and the very concept of native integrity created a climate of fear on reservations. The National Congress of American Indians, or NCAI, formed in 1944, took a leading role in opposing termination. In a letter written to the NCAI in 1947, Amy Hallingstad, Tlingit, voiced her concern:

Left: Secretary of the Interior Julius A. Krug found a photo opportunity when he pledged his support to the improvement of Navajo schools, hospitals, and way of life.

Below: An Inuit fishing camp near Cape Nome, Alaska.

"We have decided the real reason why our possessions are being taken from us is that we are human beings and not wolves or bears. The men from Washington have set aside many millions of acres on which wolves and bears may not be disturbed and nobody objects to that."

—AMY HALLINGSTAD, TLINGIT

We have decided the real reason why our possessions are being taken from us is that we are human beings and not wolves or bears. The men from Washington have set aside many millions of acres on which wolves and bears may not be disturbed and nobody objects to that. Perhaps if we were wolves and bears we could have as much protection. But we are only human beings. There are no closed seasons when it comes to skinning Alaska Natives.

Congress formally implemented the reservation termination policy in 1953. Under Public Law 280, state agencies would take over federal services and jurisdiction and the local role of the

Right: *A visiting doctor declared children of this Seminole reservation "30 percent healthier than white children."*

Below: *Brushing and flossing: the imposed method of personal hygiene.*

IRA-based tribal councils. After termination, native Americans would no longer be recognized as such by federal, state, or local governments.

For their part, many young war veterans found their reservations in worse shape than when they had left. Having seen the world and new material comforts, they resisted a return to poverty. Many eagerly accepted the relocation program's offers, expecting to assimilate happily into mid-century America. The reality, for most, was very different: relocation exchanged rural for urban poverty among hostile strangers. For those accustomed to a totally different environment, urban ghettos came as a culture shock. Watt Spade, a Cherokee storyteller, described a visit to one such ghetto in the 1950s:

One time I went up there to Chicago where my brother lives.…We were a little hungry so we stopped to eat on the way across town. This restaurant we stopped at was all glass on the outside, like one big window. You could see all the people eating inside. They weren't sitting down, either; they were all standing up at a counter that wound all around through the place. They were standing along both sides of this counter, but they didn't seem to be talking to each other or looking at each other. It was like they were all looking at the

Voting Rights

Only a handful of native American tribes had gained the right to vote in federal elections before 1900, primarily through treaties. Not until 1924 did all native Americans obtain both citizenship and the right to vote in national elections. However, many states and municipalities barred them from voting on grounds of prejudice, "legalized" by the argument that they paid no property tax on reservation lands. It took Federal Court rulings across several decades to bring about scenes like the one above, in which Seminole Indians cast their ballots in a Miami, Florida, referendum.

In Gallup, New Mexico, Navajo John Idasa could not register to vote (right) until 1948 due to restrictive state laws. As Ed Boyer, a Shoshone-Bannock resident of Idaho's Fort Hall Reservation explained in the 1950s: "It is hard to get our people to vote: [They] have been told so many things, and promised so many things that didn't work out, that they don't take any interest in an election."

Right: *Two boys from Carcross, in the Yukon, look out to a future that remains unclear.*

Opposite: *The stereotypes caricatured in "The Red Man and The White Man" distinguished at least one characteristic that was more than skin deep.*

Below: *The convenience of the car and conventional medicine made the difference between life and death for this baby with pneumonia, when a Navajo medicine man called in local health workers. What price penicillin?*

wall....Finally I said I didn't think I was ready to settle down there just yet. We went on back to the bus station and waited around for the bus back to Oklahoma.

In 1947 the Bureau of Indian Affairs recommended a list of tribes deemed ready for termination—that is, no longer needing government assistance to survive. The Menominee, a Wisconsin-based tribe with a successful lumber business, headed the list. In 1951 the tribe was awarded $7.6 million as compensation for BIA mismanagement earlier in the century, with the stipulation that they agree to termination. When termination came in 1961, after some stalling on the part of tribal leaders, the tribe was reorganized into a corporation and the members became shareholders. The reservation became a county. The Menominee corporation was subjected to restrictions never placed on non-native corporations. They could not take out a mortgage on their property. They were supervised by a board of local businessmen, and the majority of shares in their trust fund was controlled by local bankers. The settlement money was soon exhausted in payments for taxes and services, and the Menominee went into a decline. Then they began a long struggle to have their federal trust relationship and their reservation restored. By 1958 Congress had decided not to terminate any tribe against its will. Finally, in 1973, the Menominee won the repeal of their termination act.

In Canada, too, there was little improvement for the First Nations in the first half of the twentieth century, a period in which the impact of the 1876 Indian Act was still being felt. Volunteering for active duty in two world wars did not even bring natives the right to travel freely within the country they had served—they were required to carry a government pass until the latter half of the century. Change would soon follow on both sides of the border.

"As I look around at the Indian situation, it looks like one big seething cauldron about ready to explode."

—ROBERT K. THOMAS,
CHEROKEE

In the late 1950s and the 1960s, African Americans intensified their push for civil rights. Unlike other persons of color, however, native Americans had not pressed for inclusion in the mainstream. As Vine Deloria, Jr., would phrase it, what Indians wanted was a "leave us alone policy" that would allow them to work out their own destinies without government bureaucracies dictating the terms. However, problems of discrimination, police brutality, unemployment, and past injustices remained pressing. As Cherokee scholar Robert K. Thomas observed in 1964: "As I look around at the Indian situation, it looks like one big seething cauldron about ready to explode."

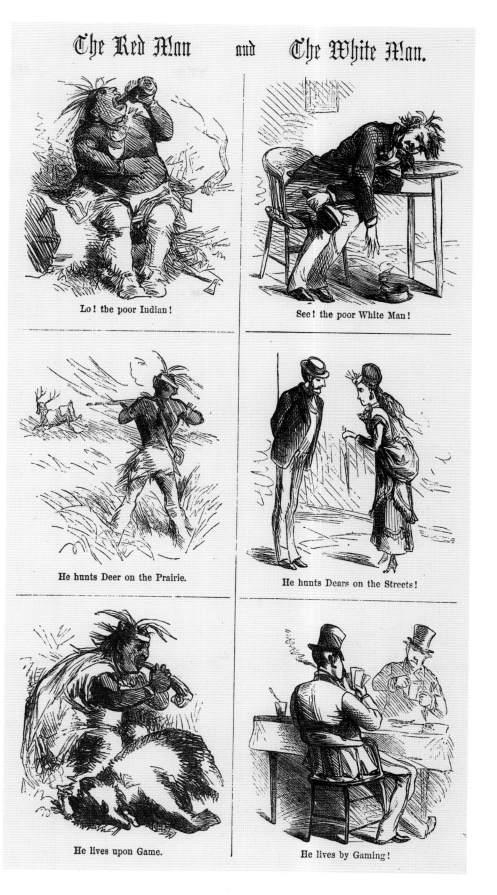

The Red Man and The White Man.

Lo! the poor Indian!

See! the poor White Man!

He hunts Deer on the Prairie.

He hunts Dears on the Streets!

He lives upon Game.

He lives by Gaming!

Renewal

"With all things and in all things, we are relatives."

—Sioux Proverb

Opposite: *An Eskimo family reconciles elements of a traditional heritage with comforts of the twentieth century.*

Below: *Many members of the newly politicized "hippie generation" adapted native American motifs to identify themselves as a "counterculture."*

With the 1960s came widespread social change across the continent and across all ethnic lines. The distinction between political and personal blurred, especially among the young; authority and the values of the establishment were challenged and rejected. "Hippies," or flower children, were in bloom. Longhaired and beaded, some of these '60s children ventured out to the reservations to "drop out" and be "at one" with the Indians, attracted to what they perceived as an alternative to prevailing social rules.

From ancient prophecies, the Hopi, one of the most conservative of all the native nations, anticipated a time when white children would be ready to listen seriously to native ways. But, according to Hopi Peter Nuvamsa, Sr., "Those hippies offended our way of life." They saw in the native lifeways only what they wanted to see—freedom and a lack of materialism— but they did not respect the traditions, rules and responsibilities of the Hopi way. Nevertheless, for the first time since the "noble savage" concept was popularized at the turn of the century, many Americans were looking to their indigenous neighbors with admiration instead of dismissal or outright contempt.

Change was about to sweep through the reservations just as it was coming to the university campuses, workplaces, and town halls of the continent, but it would come as a result of the culmination of decades of native American activism, rather than the indulgent interest of the new, socially conscious youth.

During the early and middle decades of the twentieth century, political rights groups had worked steadily and quietly to redress the wrongs of the reservation years, building a base on which more militant activists of the 1960s would take their stand. The Society of American Indians was founded in 1911 as a forum for discussion and advocacy for native people. Its members met, debated, and published influential articles. In 1944, the National

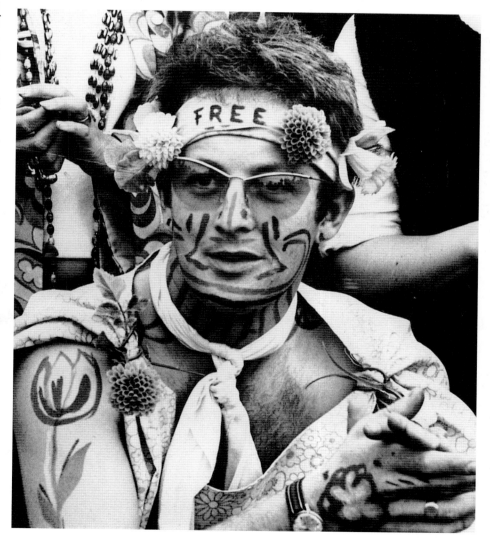

Above: *A hippie has her face painted: "flower power."*

Right: *After an attempt to set up a native American cultural center ended in the arrest of almost half of the 160 protestors, fellow-demonstrator Jane Fonda condemned the authorities at a press conference. The 1960s and '70s saw many famous personalities aligning themselves with those who challenged the establishment.*

National Congress formed the National Indian Youth Council (NIYC). Joining the young and college educated were those who had been relocated from reservations to the slums of America's great cities. Members participated in direct action, such as the "fish-in" protests conducted in Washington State by a group that pressed for recognition of a century-old treaty. In 1974 a federal court decision would hold that native people were entitled to one-half of the harvestable fish in dispute. This decision would not come without a decade-long fight, both legal and physical.

By the 1960s, politicians were openly acknowledging that liquidating Indian reservations had been a bad idea. The Kennedy administration repudiated the policies of termination and relocation, but by 1960 more than 30 percent of native Americans already lived outside of reservations; by 1970 that figure would rise to 50 percent. Like members of other minorities, many of those who experienced urban poverty and discrimination began to fight back.

On the reservations, too, there were compelling reasons to protest. By 1964 Senecas in upper New York State were outraged over the flooding of their valley by the Kinzua Dam project, which violated one of the oldest treaties with the United States. In Washington State game wardens stepped up their arrests of fish-

Congress of American Indians (NCAI) was founded in Denver by Indian leaders who subscribed to John Collier's style of self-government for tribes, as developed under the 1934 Indian Reorganization Act. The NCAI played a major role in mobilizing Indians against hostile legislation.

During the 1960s, the momentum increased. In 1960 college-educated youth who wanted a more radical stance than that taken by the

ermen who insisted on exercising their treaty water rights. The use of peyote cactus in sacred rituals had come under new legal assault in California. In Alaska and northern Canada, the Inuit were facing water-rights challenges. A mood of resistance and insistence on self-determination was spreading and gaining strength.

AIMing For Change

Founded in 1968, the American Indian Movement (AIM) originated as a response to conditions in urban Minneapolis in what Vernon Bellecourt, Ojibwa, described as "the Indian ghetto community," where "everything was deteriorating....There was police harassment and brutality." Frustrated with "white, do-gooder" solutions, Vernon's brother Clyde Bellecourt and other activists established the native-run nonprofit corporation. "I tried to work within the System for four years, demanding a fair share of it for my people," said Clyde Bellecourt, quoted in Peter Matthiessen's classic account of AIM activities, *In The Spirit of Crazy Horse* (1983):

> But all the money was controlled by the churches and bureaucracies, and they weren't interested in any programs that might have led toward real economic independence for the Indians. Our movement was based on the guarantees to Indians in all the treaties; we didn't want to get caught up in the civil-rights struggle because that was between blacks and whites; it was within the System, and the System had nothing to do with Indians.

With backing from some local churches, the "AIM patrol" was established: by monitoring police radios, often arriving at the scene of an alleged crime before the police, the patrol worked hard to reduce police brutality and arrests, as well as to inform those who were arrested of their basic rights. The AIM patrol produced immediate results. For twenty-two consecutive weekends, no native Americans were arrested in Minneapolis, a success noted in *Time* magazine.

AIM soon began to focus on wider, nonlocal issues as well, among them self-determination and sovereignty, and increasing the level

Left: AIM leader Russell Means opening an eight-day conference with a call to vigilance, encouraging participants to stand up and demand their lawful rights.

Below: (Left to right) Reverend Ben Chavis, Clyde Bellecourt, and Angela Davis announce their intent to form a broadly based organization "against racial and political repression."

"Anywhere Indians are standing up for themselves...that's where you'll find the American Indian Movement."

—RUSSELL MEANS, AIM LEADER

Right: *Onlookers survey the scene at Alcatraz Island, the former federal penitentiary, shortly after the occupation by AIM demonstrators brought international attention to both the site and their cause.*

of awareness of the rich heritage of the native nations—a heritage that had all but disappeared for many urban Indians. Members looked outside the ghetto to such spiritual authorities as Leonard Crow Dog, a Lakota medicine man, to learn about native traditions and obtain guidance. Crow Dog told them:

To be an Indian is to be spiritual....We have the spirituality, yet we are warriors. We'll stand up and fight for our people. We haven't had that for many years. The warrior class of this century is bound by the bond of the drum....That circle around the drum brings us together.

Among the leaders of the new organization were Clyde Bellecourt, elected national director; Dennis Banks, an Ojibwa who lived in Minneapolis; and Russell Means, an Oglala Lakota who had grown up mostly in California but spent part of his boyhood on the South Dakota reservation. In the 1960s, Means had worked as director of the Cleveland Indian Center. Like the militant Black Panthers, these leaders shared a desire to use direct action to force their issues into the public eye. AIM members visited reservations and cities across the country to exhort young people to reclaim their pride, and new chapters were soon being formed.

"The American Indian Movement hit our reservation like a tornado, like a new wind blowing out of nowhere, a drumbeat from far off, getting louder and louder."

—MARY CROW DOG, LAKOTA

AIM's first widely publicized action was its dramatic takeover of Alcatraz Island, in San Francisco Bay, in November 1969. A group of seventy-eight staged a night landing and claimed the former prison site as their own, releasing the following statement:

PROCLAMATION TO THE GREAT WHITE FATHER AND ALL HIS PEOPLE: We, the native Americans, reclaim the land known as Alcatraz Island in the name of all American Indians by right of discovery.

We wish to be fair and honorable in our dealings with the Caucasian inhabitants of the land, and hereby offer the following treaty:

We will purchase said Alcatraz Island for twenty-four dollars in glass beads and red cloth, a precedent set by the white man's purchase of a similar island [Manhattan] about 300 years ago....We will give to the inhabitants of this island a portion of the land...to be held in trust... for as long as the sun shall rise and the rivers go down to the sea. We will offer [the inhabitants] our religion, our education, our life-ways, in order to help them achieve our level of civilization and thus raise them and all their white brothers up from their savage and unhappy state....

We feel that this...island is more than suitable for an Indian reservation...by the white man's own standards...in that:

1. It is isolated from modern facilities, and without adequate means of transportation.

2. It has no fresh running water.

3. It has inadequate sanitation facilities.

4. There are no oil or mineral rights.

5. There is no industry and so unemployment is very great.

6. There are no health care facilities.

7. The soil is rocky and non-productive; and the land does not support game.

8. There are no educational facilities.

9. The population has always exceeded the land base.

10. The population has always been held as prisoners and kept dependent on others. Further, it would be fitting...that ships from all over the world, entering the Golden Gate, would first see Indian land.

The reaction of the alarmed authorities to the takeover was described by Adam Fortunate Eagle, an Ojibwa, as "right out of a Keystone Kop movie. Ships, motorboats, sailing yachts... all heading towards them." One newspaper headline read "Indians Invade Alcatraz; U.S. Plans Counter-Attack." The protestors occupied the island for seven months, attracting publicity—favorable and otherwise—throughout the world's media.

Other actions followed rapidly, some equally effective in gaining press attention and reminding the world of the issues hitherto left out of the history books. On Thanksgiving Day in 1970, Plymouth Rock was painted red. In 1971 a demonstration was staged at Mount Rushmore during the Fourth of July holiday, to remind Americans that the U.S. government had broken the 1868 Fort Laramie treaty with the Lakota only eight years after signing it. Part of the treaty conceded that the Black Hills belonged to the Sioux. The fact that the government had carved in their sacred rock the faces of past presidents—who had directed the seizure of native land—seemed especially offensive.

Below: One of the seventy-eight AIM members who invaded Alcatraz spells out a succinct summary of the group's message to the world.

Right: *As 500 demonstrators occupy the Bureau of Indian Affairs in Washington, D.C., a protestor wraps herself symbolically in an upside-down American flag.*

Right: *Outside the Bureau, other demonstrators, armed with makeshift defenses, stood on guard.*

The AIM protestors made their point with humor. Some managed to climb behind the enormous rock carvings. Russell Means found a special space between the heads of Roosevelt and Lincoln; while he could see the tourists below, they could not see him. The mountain amplified his voice as he shouted:

Listen, my children, HONOR THY FATHER AND MOTHER.... THOU SHALT NOT STEAL.... THOU SHALT HONOR THY TREATIES, I FORGOT THAT ONE IN MY LAST MESSAGE....

The following year AIM, in conjunction with several other Indian groups, mobilized a mass demonstration, which came to be called the "Trail of Broken Treaties." A protest for sovereignty, it took the form of a march from the West Coast to Washington, D.C., involving participants from all over America; it has been described as the greatest native American action since Little Bighorn.

The Trail of Broken Treaties culminated in the impromptu takeover of the Bureau of Indian Affairs headquarters by approximately 500 demonstrators on November 2, 1972, making

> *"They call us the New Indians. Hell, we are the Old Indians, the landlords of this continent, coming to collect the rent."*
>
> —DENNIS BANKS

Below: After the occupation, demonstrators announced they were in possession of Bureau documents that would be destroyed unless the Twenty Points were fully addressed.

front-page news during the buildup to the presidential election. The takeover started as a protest against the miserable conditions that greeted the marchers when they reached Washington. They had been promised a decent place for their elders to stay; what they got was a "rat-infested" church basement.

At the BIA building, protestors barricaded themselves inside and demanded meetings to negotiate their issues—the government's continuing failure to honor treaties and to carry out economic and social responsibilities, from education to land and tax reform to legal protections for freedom of religious expression. Their agenda was laid out in "Twenty Points," detailing items from earlier treaties that had not been executed.

The Nixon administration responded swiftly to the embarrassingly timed takeover, promising "meaningful dialogue" (although this was only to begin after election week). Overnight, police encircled the "Native American Embassy," as the protestors had renamed the building, and were met with cries of "Turn the bureau over to us....We've been listening to you for 300 years" (according to coverage in the following day's *New York Times*). After six days, the siege ended when the government appointed two senior officials to "seriously consider" the Twenty Points, and gave the protestors the money they needed to leave town. When they departed, the occupiers removed file cabinets, along with valuable objects that had been taken from reservations, and left many furnishings and fixtures damaged. The Twenty Points became lost in bad publicity. As Secretary of the Interior Rogers Morton said, "It is a shame that a small, willful band of malcontents should try to wreck the headquarters of the government's chief instrument for serving the Indian community."

The Trail of Broken Treaties

The twenty-point document prepared by AIM for the mass demonstration in Washington, D.C., in November 1972 included the following objectives:

- A comprehensive review of all treaties, including those that had not been ratified by the U.S. Congress
- Re-establishment of treaty making between tribes and the federal government
- Abolition of the Bureau of Indian Affairs
- Restoration of Indian land bases
- Protection of legal rights and religious freedoms
- A nationally televised address to the American people and a joint session of Congress
- Resubmission of unratified treaties to the U.S. Senate
- Creation of a Congressional Joint Committee on Reconstruction of Indian Relations
- Creation of an "Office of Federal Indian Relations and Community Reconstruction"
- Indian Commerce and Tax Immunities

Through good publicity and bad, such high-profile protests succeeded in attracting young members to the movement, drawn by the positive and proud stance of the leadership and encouraged by their victories. AIM drew attention to neglected treaties and demanded that their voices be heard.

Violence at Pine Ridge

In February 1972 an Oglala Sioux from Pine Ridge Reservation, Raymond Yellow Thunder, was killed by two white youths in nearby Gordon, Nebraska. The perpetrators were arrested, but then released without bail awaiting trial for second-degree manslaughter. The victim's family, outraged by the initial verdict of suicide and subsequently, after an autopsy, by the release of the killers, called on AIM for help. Severt Young Bear, a relative of the victim, was quoted by Peter Matthiessen describing the events precipitated by this outright failure of justice:

Raymond Yellow Thunder was an uncle of mine and his sisters all live [on Pine Ridge Reservation]....They went to the BIA for help...because they wouldn't let them see the autopsy report, and they sealed the coffin when they brought it back. This is what really hurt his sisters....So after they ran into all these brick walls, they came in crying, "Sonny, we don't have no place to turn....You have some friends that are with AIM....We want a full investigation."

AIM led 1,000 Sioux demonstrators in a caravan of 200 cars to Gordon, where authorities had to capitulate to their demands. This victory gained AIM greater respect in the eyes of traditionalists at Pine Ridge, who had thus far (like many other reservation-based native Americans) regarded the radical "city Indians" with suspicion.

In January 1973, in a similar episode of mindless violence in the area, Wesley Bad Heart Bull was stabbed in a Buffalo Gap bar by a white businessman, Darold Schmidt. Again, the perpetrator was charged only with involuntary manslaughter, but Sarah Bad Heart Bull, Wesley's mother, took the case to AIM, whose leaders joined more than two hundred locals in a march to the courthouse in Custer, in the Black Hills, to demand justice. A riot broke out when Mrs. Bad Heart Bull was refused entry and in the melee, an abandoned building next to the courthouse was set on fire. The Custer courthouse riot became a symbolic event, the first real outbreak of violence between white men and Lakota since the massacre at Wounded Knee in 1890. Afterward, sixty-five U.S. marshals were assigned to Pine Ridge to "keep the peace" in and around the reservation as the ugly tensions mounted.

Meanwhile, Pine Ridge tribal chairman Dick Wilson's impeachment hearing had been terminated. Wilson was a model tribal president, at least in BIA eyes; he kept things quiet on the reservation, cooperated fully with the authorities, and was well rewarded for his loyalty. His support team, the "Guardians of the Oglala Nation" (GOONS), helped maintain Wilson's power. AIM represented a threat to Wilson, who now declared war on them: "If Russell Means sets foot on this reservation, I, Dick Wilson, will personally cut his braids off," he warned, apparently without humor.

Below: *In a national news conference, Charles E. Trimble, executive director of the National Congress of American Indians, condemns the actions of the "Trail of Broken Treaties" activists. Trimble severed ties between the NCAI and AIM, whose use of civil disobedience tactics was not universally accepted.*

With the atmosphere of tension mounting on the reservation during the early months of 1973, Oglala chiefs, with Frank Fools Crow as their spokesman, solicited AIM's help and representation in addressing the violence and other problems. A meeting was held near Pine Ridge, during which residents decided on a symbolic confrontation with the authorities that was to take place at Wounded Knee, where almost 250 Sioux had been massacred in 1890. At the site, they issued a statement demanding hearings on the 1868 treaty guaranteeing Sioux lands and an investigation of the BIA, which read in part:

The only two options open to the United States of America are 1) They wipe out the old people, women, children, and men, by shooting and attacking us. 2) they negotiate our demands.

"We hold the Knee!"

—AIM PROTESTOR, 1973

Wounded Knee Revisited

On February 28, 1973, several hundred Lakota Sioux, along with AIM supporters from across the country, took over the hamlet of Wounded Knee and declared it Indian Country. Almost immediately, the tiny community was surrounded by forces in armored personnel carriers and circled by surveillance helicopters.

Madonna Gilbert, a cousin of Russell Means, recalled in an interview that no one had expected the demonstration to last for seventy-one days.

We figured we'd be there just two or three days, we were never told to bring food or anything. I just had my jacket and my purse! And my two kids! We didn't realize what was happening until we were surrounded. I mean helicopters, APCs, the whole Vietnam number, blue jump suits, infrared lights, guns everywhere you looked; it was Wounded Knee and the Seventh Cavalry all over again.

As the police arrived in force, the protestors took eleven people hostage, adding considerably to the stakes. As time went on,

Below: *AIM members in militant attitude: At Wounded Knee, protestors armed with rifles stand guard outside the occupied Sacred Heart Catholic Church, where eleven hostages were being held.*

"I am not afraid to die. If I die at Wounded Knee I will go where Crazy Horse and Sitting Bull and our grandfathers are."

—LEONARD CROW DOG

Above: *The trading post at Wounded Knee was taken over as AIM's headquarters for the duration of the siege.*

Right: *Five of the eleven hostages taken during the AIM action. "Gildersleeve [seated at left] had always tried to exploit the site of our greatest tragedy, making it into a tourist attraction," one participant commented. Wilbur Riegert, at far right, believed that the besieged demonstrators were "the real hostages."*

Opposite: *During the protracted occupation, traditional rites sustained the determination of the demonstrators. "Looking back, I really believed that the broken hoop was mended at Wounded Knee, and that the water was being given to the tree of life," Dennis Banks remembered later.*

though, it appeared that even some of the hostages themselves were sympathetic to the Lakota claims. One of them, Guy Fritze, said to a *Newsweek* reporter two weeks into the siege: "We are free to come and go as we wish. We are treated fine. We were not really forced, and I think it is worth it. I believe these fellas have got a story to tell." Eighty-two-year-old Wilbur Riegert, another hostage, later said, "We as a group of hostages decided to stay on to save AIM and our property. Had we not, those troops would have come down here and killed all these people. The real hostages are the AIM people."

Demonstrators were, indeed, effectively trapped and had not arrived prepared for their prolonged encampment. Mary Crow Dog, who was pregnant during the siege, even gave birth during the conflict, and described her harrowing experience in her autobiographical account *Lakota Woman* (1991):

I had my first baby during a firefight, with the bullets crashing through one wall and coming out through the other. When my newborn son was only a day old and the marshals really opened up on us, I wrapped him up in a blanket and ran for it…pray-

ing "It's all right if I die, but please let him live." When I came out of Wounded Knee I was not even healed up, but they put me in jail at Pine Ridge and took my baby away.

Although there were heavy bursts of fire at times throughout the stand-off, only two people, protestors Frank Clearwater and Buddy Lamont, were killed. The latter was memorialized with the following inscription on his tombstone, a monument erected near the mass grave of those massacred in 1890: "Two thousand came to Wounded Knee in 1973. One stayed."

Despite the militant stance of the protest and the negative publicity caused by the taking of hostages, the military's heavy-handed actions aroused more sympathy for the protesters than had been anticipated. In negotiating an end to the siege, the government promised that leaders of the takeover would not be prosecuted. The amnesty was, however, short-lived, and charges were soon filed against those perceived to be the ringleaders.

> ## "Two thousand came to Wounded Knee in 1973. One stayed."
>
> —TOMBSTONE OF PROTESTOR

The prosecution team restricted the movements of AIM leaders Dennis Banks and Russell Means during much of the next few years. Their trial was transferred to St. Paul, Minnesota, where it opened in January 1974; they were portrayed as common criminals who had terrorized and looted a helpless community. The defense, referring to the 1868 treaty, presented them as political prisoners. In the end, after eight months, the jury ruled "not guilty" on a count of conspiracy, and the judge dismissed the charges of larceny and assault. On the FBI's behavior, including its manipulation of evidence, the judge delivered a more damning verdict: "It's hard for me to believe that the FBI, which I have revered for so long, has stooped so low."

"I'm Not a Mascot"

Another American institution—football—came under assault at the 1992 Superbowl in Minneapolis, where AIM protestors turned out in force to object to the team name and mascot of the Washington Redskins. The protestors demanded an end to "Sports' Racism," continuing a long campaign against the patronizing appropriation and misuse of native American names and icons, especially in leisure and advertising. "Pride" was the campaign's watchword.

The 1973 Wounded Knee confrontation had wide ramifications and exacerbated long-running disputes within the Indian community over political protest tactics and goals. While many native activists (especially supporters of AIM) favored direct action as the only means to real change, others took a less militant approach. Steps toward reconciliation between supporters of the opposing approaches were gradually achieved through the work of lawyers whose attention to treaty rights spoke to the concerns of both groups.

Meanwhile, a wave of violence spread across the Pine Ridge Reservation. AIM members described Wilson and the GOONS as conducting a "reign of terror" against them—and anyone suspected of sympathizing with AIM. For a time, quiet, rural Shannon County had the highest murder rate in America. And harassment of the Lakota community by the FBI (evidence of which Amnesty International later described as amounting to "proof") finally provoked yet another violent confrontation.

The Leonard Peltier Case

AIM leaders maintained a presence at Pine Ridge during the turbulent aftermath of the Wounded Knee confrontation. Several members, including Leonard Peltier, were encamped at the Jumping Bull Ranch when a shootout occurred on June 26, 1975, in which two FBI agents were killed. The agents had reportedly been chasing a van in pursuit of someone they were attempting to arrest. They followed it into the Jumping Bull compound. Norman Brown was in the AIM camp that day:

All of a sudden a whole bunch of shooting started. All the guys took off and went up the hill to find out what was going on, because there were about four different families living up there, and all of them had young children....By the time we hit that main road, there was already a roadblock on it, and a lot of people there. And I was so surprised because it seemed like the shooting had just barely started and already they had roadblocks up.

Their encampment nearly surrounded, AIM members fled. Leonard Peltier remembered:

> ## "After centuries of murder…could I have been wise in thinking that you would break that tradition and commit an act of justice?"
>
> —LEONARD PELTIER

"We all sat down together and said a prayer. If the Great Spirit will help us, we'll get out safely; if not, we're going to die." Norman Brown recalled that an eagle alighted in a tree above their heads and screamed. "We expected to be killed…we were surrounded…but an eagle came and sat in a tree above us and then flew away, and we knew that was the direction we should go in."

The fugitives managed to escape, but two of them, Dino Butler and Bob Robideaux, were later apprehended and put on trial for the shootings. They were acquitted, claiming self-defense. Peltier, however, was not so fortunate; he reached Canada, but was extradited and tried in Fargo, North Dakota. The trial judge ruled that the events leading up to the shootout, the historical background of Pine Ridge violence, and the persecution of AIM by the FBI, were inadmissible as evidence. The jury took six hours to deliberate, and found Peltier guilty on two counts of murder in the first degree. Before sentencing, Peltier addressed the court:

After centuries of murder…could I have been wise in thinking that you would break that tradition and commit an act of justice?…No, I'm not the guilty one here; I'm not the one who should be called a criminal—white racist America is the criminal for the destruction of our lands and my people; to hide your guilt from the decent human beings in America and around the world, you will sentence me to two consecutive life terms without any hesitation.

Today, after serving some twenty years of those terms, Leonard Peltier remains in prison, although rights groups around the world have spoken on his behalf. Documents relating to the case have been kept secret.

From Alcatraz to Washington to Wounded Knee, AIM's activities and tactics met with conflicting responses. While the bravery of the warriors, as AIM members were popularly perceived within sympathetic communities, inspired many of the young to believe in themselves again, other native Americans did not feel comfortable with confrontation, as noted in the comments of Ojibwa novelist Gerald Vizenor:

Below: *Leonard Peltier is escorted to a waiting helicopter, deported by order of Canadian Justice Minister Ron Basford to face murder charges across the border.*

Above: Members of the Native Youth Association join hands in a circle of solidarity outside the Peace Tower on Ottawa's Parliament Hill.

Right: George Manuel, President of Canada's National Indian Brotherhood, announced his dissent on behalf of numerous groups at a 1974 press conference after an agreement between the James Bay Cree and the Quebec government.

Behind the scenes, tribal people have been arguing about the use of violence as a means of change. Some say that violence has only polarized the dominant white society and strained interpersonal relationships. Other tribal people argue that violence has made the job of moderates working within the system much easier. White people listen better after violence.

If AIM's tactics were controversial, their results were beyond doubt. In addition to placing native American issues firmly on the national agenda, the organization kindled a new sense of pride in a generation that had almost lost touch with its spiritual heritage, and helped revive the ancestral traditions and beliefs that had been driven underground for a century.

During the 1960s and '70s, parallel with the rise of AIM, Canada's native peoples also pursued tribal sovereignty and self-determination issues while joining forces to consolidate on their common grievances. In 1968—an explosive year south of the border, marked by AIM's founding, the assassinations of Dr. Martin Luther King, Jr. and Senator Robert Kennedy, and rioting in many U.S. cities—the Parti Québeçois was established, to pursue separatist goals for Quebec's French-speaking population. Political debate and anti-authority sentiment increased through the next few years. Native groups continued their own challenges to the legitimacy of Canadian government, through demonstration and legal work on unresolved treaty issues.

Ottawa was the scene of ongoing protests on issues ranging from tribal land ownership to membership in the United Nations. Young people of the Native Youth Association rallied in front of the Peace Tower on Parliament Hill

Left: *Kahn-Tineta Horn, a high-profile activist and former model, speaking out in 1964 during a dispute with Canada's National Indian Council.*

Left: *Demonstrators from the Caughnawaga Reservation in 1973, protesting the Canadian government's repeated violation of treaties.*

Opposite, above: *Proclaiming the "Spirit of South Moresby Island," demonstrators protest logging in British Columbia.*

Opposite, below: *A Miwok medicine man's powerful gesture of opposition to proposed construction on a sacred burial site.*

Below: *The world's largest open-pit uranium operation, the Jackpile Mine in Anaconda, New Mexico. The mine was closed down in 1982 after sustained pressure by environmentalists—especially those whose reservation it polluted.*

in the summer of 1973 after a 24-hour occupation of the Indian Affairs Building. Members of the Iroquois Nation picketed to protest that "The Aim of the Indian Act is Genocide!" and to exhort Parliament to "Renew Violated Iroquois Treaties." George Manuel, president of the National Indian Brotherhood, spoke on behalf of several Quebec activist groups in 1974 to say that their members could not confirm an agreement between the James Bay Cree and the Quebec government without betraying their own people. The Inuit stepped up their campaign for self-determination in Nunavut, their home territory. All over Canada, as in the United States, a pan-Indian movement was gathering strength, as native Americans rose above tribal differences to forge a common identity.

Reclaiming Land and Faith
While native American activism in the 1970s centered around treaty rights and other legal issues, there was also a deeper cultural struggle underway. Russell Means, who had obtained a

college degree before serving time in prison for "rioting to obstruct justice" in 1973, continued his studies behind bars. In a speech delivered before the Black Hills Survival Gathering in 1980, he summarized his criticisms of "white" thinking with the observation:

Newton [reduced] the physical universe to a linear mathematical equation. Descartes did the same thing with culture. John Locke did it with politics, and Adam Smith did it with economics. Each one of these "thinkers" took a piece of the spirituality of human existence and converted it into a code, an abstraction….Each of these intellectual revolutions served to abstract the European mentality even further, to remove the wonderful complexity and spirituality from the universe and replace it with a logical sequence: one, two, three… Answer!

Across the cultural divide, native American rights were, by the 1970s, being asserted by people who understood the "white man's"

system better than ever before—through their experiences with reservation education or city life; through rough treatment at the hands of, or integration into, "the system"; and through increasing attention to the media. Activists had also made significant progress in reclaiming and reinterpreting traditional wisdom and spirituality. Nowhere would the traditional messages speak more strongly than on land issues—on the right to inhabit, respect, and live with the land without interference. Legal work within the context of treaty rights proved fruitful and the Trail of Broken Treaties and Wounded Knee actions had brought new impetus. While the ultimate goal of these actions was sovereignty and self-determination, many less publicized cases concentrated on environmental issues.

"No European can ever teach a Lakota to be a Lakota, a Hopi to be Hopi."

—RUSSELL MEANS

Native American spiritual leaders have long passed on traditions of reverence for the land. One of the most quoted elders, Chief Seattle, Dwamish, had said in the late nineteenth century: "Every part of all this soil is sacred to my people. Every hillside, every valley…has been hallowed by some sad or happy event in days long vanished." Today the same ideas resound. In an interview for the Fall 1994 issue of *Wilderness*, Bill Tall Bull, Northern Cheyenne, expressed a similar sentiment: "The earth has a spirit. All of creation has a spirit. Everything that comes from the earth is sacred."

Environmental and land-use issues often brought native Americans into direct conflict with big-business interests and expansionist economic policymakers. Pollution was one among many battlegrounds tackled by activists. Others included the protection of traditional land-use rights and of sacred sites.

Passage of the 1978 American Indian Freedom of Religion Act had enshrined in law the protection of native American faiths under the

Right: *Ancient tribal fishing grounds were rapidly and irrevocably damaged by the Dalles Dam across the Columbia River in Oregon. These before-and-after views were photographed at a five-hour interval when the dam went into operation in March 1957.*

First Amendment, but in practice, the act did not prove as effective as had been hoped. In April 1988, in *Lyng v. Northwest Indian Cemetery Protective Association*, the U.S. Supreme Court ruled that the First Amendment does not protect sacred sites from being destroyed if there is no intent to harm religious practice:

> *This case requires us to consider whether the First Amendment's Free Exercise Clause forbids the Government from permitting timber harvesting in, or constructing a road through, a portion of a National Forest that has traditionally been used for religious purposes by members of three American Indian tribes in northwestern California. We conclude that it does not.... Whatever may be the exact line between unconstitutional prohibitions on the free exercise of religion and the legitimate conduct by government of its own affairs, the location of the line cannot*

Below: *Fresh water—and fragile ecosystems—have been carelessly polluted by industry without regulation or penalty, until recently.*

> *depend on measuring the effects of a governmental action on a religious objector's spiritual development. The Government does not dispute, and we have no reason to doubt, that the logging and road building projects at issue in this case could have devastating effects on traditional Indian religious practices....However we might wish that it were otherwise, government simply could not operate if it were required to satisfy every citizen's religious needs and desires.*

In dissent, Justice William J. Brennan argued strongly that the decision "makes a mockery" of the First Amendment. In one of the most decisively pro-native American statements made by a Supreme Court justice, he wrote:

> *I find it difficult...to imagine conduct more insensitive to religious needs than the Government's determination to build a marginally useful road in the face of uncontradicted evidence that the road will render the practice of respondents' religion impossible. Nor do I believe that respondents will derive any solace from the knowledge that although the practice of their religions will become "more difficult" as a result of the Government's actions, they remain free to maintain their religious beliefs. Given today's ruling, that freedom amounts to nothing more than the right to believe that their religion will be destroyed.*

The Supreme Court's ruling resulted in a series of devastating losses around America's reservations. Among those whose sacred sites were threatened were the San Carlos Apache, along the Gila River, and the Havasupai of Arizona, whose revered Red Butte was developed for uranium processing.

Left and below: Workers in the Port of Valdez, Alaska, begin their arduous task of limiting the damage to Prince William Sound after the disastrous Exxon Valdez oil spill. Disasters make headlines, but opposition to routine pollution and unsafe industrial practice has been limited to the domain of the few who share the native American respect for the natural world. Hobart Keith, Lakota Sioux, posed the question: "Let me ask you this—why are there only 8 inches of top soil left in America, when there once were some 187 inches at the time of the Declaration of Independence in 1776? Where goes our sacred earth?"

Many sites considered sacred had long ago acquired that status through their natural properties, either as unusually shaped features or outstandingly beautiful or peaceful places. Walter Echo Hawk (Pawnee), attorney with the Native American Rights Fund, Boulder, Colorado, said in a 1994 interview: "Native American sacred sites…happen to rank among the most breathtaking natural wonders left in America. There's a sense of great sadness and urgency within the Native community as they have to stand by and watch these sites being destroyed." Once defiled, these sacred places caused untold distress to the communities that had held them in such awe.

By the later decades of the twentieth century, boundaries marking reservation land could no longer exclude the problems of the neighboring society. Pollution spilled over into reservations from nearby industrial sites, causing widespread environmental damage. Many conflicts, however, were not as simple

Right: *Archaeologists unearthing ancient palisades at the Cahokia Mounds earthwork—the largest on the continent—near East St. Louis, Illinois. The mounds were built by people of the Temple Mound culture of the lower Mississippi Valley, dating from c. AD 900. The site was abandoned, for unknown reasons, long before Europeans settled on the continent.*

as native American resistance to environmental abuse by unscrupulous industrial giants. Concern for environmental protection began to grow dramatically in a newly aware population at large, and the growing environmental consciousness of legislators and lobbying groups led to tightening controls that would, ironically, encroach on traditional native practices. Local and state authorities also contested reservation "privileges" for clearly economic reasons: Why should natives have a preferential right to natural resources? In 1971 Michigan abolished the distinction in its game laws between enforcement of cases involving native and non-native hunters. While the impetus for their new policy came from the threat to the trout population of Lake Superior, native Americans were infuriated by the lack of respect for their need-based fishing practice, as sport fishing—on a scale far more damaging to the trout population—was suddenly granted equal status and the activities of both groups were controlled under recreational regulations.

In the Pacific Northwest, environmental lobbyists attempted to obtain regulation of logging practices, to protect the ecosystem of forested areas. This led to protest from the local logging communities who saw their livelihood threatened. Environmentalists in this case depicted both native American and logging-community claims as selfish in the context of a changing natural balance. For the native population, the irony of having the earth "saved" by the society that had done so much to destroy it was provocative in the extreme; it added considerable fuel to self-determination drives. Local tribes had respected and sustained their natural resources—like native people across the continent, whether on their ancestral homelands or in new environments after relocation—for many centuries.

Also in the Pacific Northwest, the status of salmon fishing reached crisis during the 1980s. The most significant damage to the once-prolific salmon ladders had been inflicted during the building of hydroelectric power projects along the Columbia and Snake Rivers from the 1920s through the 1970s. Dams between Port-

Left: *Education Commissioner Thomas Sobel and chiefs Leon Shenadowa and Irving Powless, Jr., exchange documents in Albany, New York, guaranteeing the return of twelve wampum belts to the Onondagas. The invaluable belts contained unique records of tribal history. Reclaiming sacred and ancestral artefacts has become increasingly important to native American communities. "It's our stuff. We made it and we know best how to use it and care for it. And now we're going to get it back," commented Crow spokesman John Pretty on Top.*

land, Oregon, and the Idaho border destroyed natural ladders that had sustained the rich Chinook salmon runs. The Snake River Coho salmon was virtually extinct by the 1980s. In 1992 the Wilderness Society predicted that nine of ten species in the area would reach extinction without immediate and radical changes. The dispute over strategies to save the salmon resulted in heated clashes between native and non-native fishermen, between the U.S. and Canadian governments, and among state authorities in the region. Meanwhile, the "rights" to fish the area seemed likely to become irrelevant. Idaho governor Cecil D. Andrus, writing in *USA Today* in July 1994, commented:

It is hard to tell someone from outside the Pacific Northwest how important the salmon is to the fabric of that region. Revered by Native Americans, sought after by sport fishermen, and regarded as a cash crop by an entire industry, the salmon is a symbol of the independence of the people who live here....The silver and red fish...became icons in the Native American culture. The salmon was carved onto totem

poles and celebrated in ancient songs, and, for centuries, was the sustaining source of food for the people. Today, the legend is nearly all that is left.

Land-rights issues are destined to remain hotly contested as a new century dawns, but the tide of environmental devastation at the hands of industry appears to have turned. At last, native American values of respect for the fragile earth have been at least partially adopted by the non-native population. Toxic waste and unbridled expansion at the expense of open land are no longer tolerated.

The Cultural Renaissance
Since the heyday of the American Indian Movement, a sense of pride in native heritage has blossomed and grown. The market for native American art has risen out of sight; in Santa Fe, New Mexico, collectors congregate each year to view selections in jewelry, painting, and stone. New Agers are drawn to the spirituality and wisdom of native cultures to perhaps an even greater degree than the hippies of the 1960s—and an appreciation of the

Right: Selling crafts, traditional and otherwise: outside the Palace of the Governors, a tourist destination in Santa Fe, New Mexico.

environmental concerns and traditional beliefs of native Americans is shared by a substantial proportion of the American and Canadian populations, rather than just those seeking "alternative" cultural values.

Many want to enjoy the fruits of the artistic and cultural traditions of native Americans, but tend not to involve themselves in the hard work of supporting native sovereignty. This attitude angers many native Americans, who bristle at the appropriation of their culture; they see this "borrowing" of art and religion as the very last invasion by the non-native. Many of the artistic treasures appropriated in earlier decades have ended up in museums where they are seen almost exclusively by non-native visitors.

Simply stated, there are many miles between sophisticated urban centers like Manhattan and most American Indians. In most museums, American Indian art, regardless of how contemporary it may be, has in the past been relegated to the natural history wings, and

Below: A visitor stops to admire sled dog pups on a visit to the Inuit trading post on Banks Island.

most of the non-Indian audience has accepted that situation. In many museums, a 300-year-old Navajo pot can be placed beside a 1994 Lakota-Sioux painting with no distinction made between the two. American Indian art has always been trapped in a kind of void.

While museum collections are seen by some as controversial, they have undoubtedly contributed to the burgeoning international interest in native American culture. Tourism and the sale of arts and crafts provide enormous economic support to many tribes. Their tra-

ditional and more modern arts are now highly prized and sold to enthusiastic collectors around the world.

The members of the Ramah Navajo Weavers Association, a cooperative of forty members spanning five generations, view their art as a prayer and their craft as a way of life, but they also understand marketing. When going through non-Indian distributors, they had once received around one-fifth of the value of their coveted creations. Now they not only breed and raise the sheep, color

the wool with natural dyes, and design the hand-woven rugs, but sell them as well—for very high prices.

Artistic treasures, however, form only one aspect of the museum and artefacts discussions. Over the past one hundred years, attitudes of curators and anthropologists toward native peoples have evolved. Unlike the days when a Franz Boas could order up an Eskimo for observation at the American Museum of Natural History, museums across the country are working today to return ancestral bones and sacred objects to their rightful places, and anthropologists are focusing on helping native peoples in their efforts to preserve their heritage. Museums with substantial native American holdings are generally run with highly sensitive attitudes toward their collections and

Above: *Modern Hopi pottery, now highly prized as fine art by the wider community, crafted by artisans in Arizona according to traditional methods. In the words of a Hopi proverb: "What should it matter that one bowl is dark and the other pale, if each is of good design and serves its purpose well?"*

Right: *A contemporary Navajo rug in the Yei style, incorporating three centuries of experience in the art of weaving.*

Left: *Colorful contemporary Navajo baskets, after a style originally used for a variety of functions, including water carrying.*

the tribes that created the artefacts. An outstanding example is Vancouver's Museum of Anthropology, housed in a modern building whose design reflects the style of traditional native communal buildings in the region. The museum displays a wide range of local native American artefacts and presents the indigenous population's history in a sensitive and accessible manner.

The National Museum of the American Indian, or First People, has, ironically, been allocated the last available space on the mall in Washington, D.C. Native Americans have taken a leading role in the planning and the current running of the museum. Poet Sherman Alexie (Coeur d'Alene) commented on the opening of the Heye Center, the Museum's New York division, in a 1994 *New York Times* article:

I celebrate the opening of the Heye Center of the National Museum of the American Indian, even as I wish there weren't a need for such a museum. I celebrate the National Museum's potential….I hope the millions of people who visit the United States Holocaust Memorial Museum in Washington will also

Below: *A selection of native American handicrafts for sale to tourists, featuring intricate beading and quillwork.*

visit the National Museum of the American Indian and come to understand how much the two places have in common.

The cultural renaissance of native American art, faith, and spirituality is also evidenced by Hollywood's recent fascination with the traditions of indigenous peoples. The cowboys-and-Indians genre of earlier times made way for the enormously successful *Dances with Wolves*, while a generation of children were offered a new interpretation on the story of Pocahontas, courtesy of the Disney studios (with the voice of Powhatan done by Russell Means). While Hollywood has always glamorized and distorted reality, these and other successes are indicative of a deeper change in North American attitudes.

Right: *New York State troopers at the Regis (Mohawk) Indian Reservation casino after violence broke out in 1990. Gaming has been a mixed blessing on reservations across the USA.*

Shifting Population, Shifting Fortunes

The twentieth century has seen demographic changes in the native and non-native populations of the United States and Canada almost as sweeping as those of the previous century. In the United States, the Bureau of the Census recorded the total native American population for 1990 as 1,959,000, with 552 federally recognized tribes (224 of them Alaskan) speaking 250 languages. Some 78 percent were recorded as living in urban areas, compared with 22 percent on reservations. Canada's 1986 native population was 711,270. These figures represent a reversal of nineteenth-century trends. Population lows are thought to have occurred around the turn of the century. Although accurate statistics are not available and estimates vary widely, the combined indigenous population of the continent was perhaps lower than two million at that time. Meanwhile, large-scale immigration to the United States and Canada continued well into the century. The economic experience of the many ethnic groups has varied widely.

The per capita income of native Americans is, at this century's end, a little less than half that of the average American, according to statistics used in a recent Scholastic report. Unemployment is more than twice the average; poverty three times the average. Almost 10 percent of native Americans are now college graduates; for the U.S. as a whole, that figure was 20.3 percent in 1990. The high school graduation rate for native Americans is 65 percent, compared with the American average of 75 percent.

While there have been few large-scale returns to tribal lands, there have been some notable exceptions, particularly on those reservations that have been successful in the gaming industry, which has generated the wealth, jobs, and housing to attract their members home. The Mashantucket Pequot of eastern Connecticut,

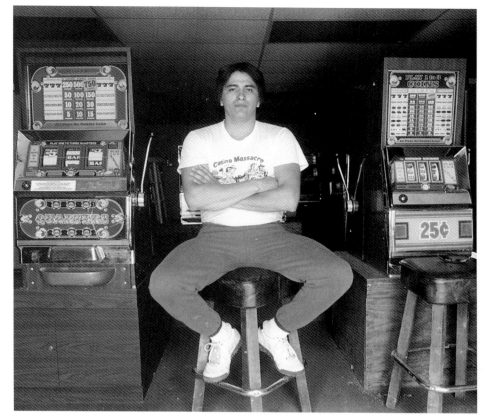

who currently run one of the most successful gaming operations in the world, are called daily by people claiming to be Pequot. The once poverty-stricken, almost entirely dispersed tribe is now able to provide housing, employment, and a tremendously high standard of living to its people. In 1994 its Foxwood Casino made a staggering $800 million, twice as much as any other casino. Gaming mogul Donald Trump, a competitor, has referred to the Pequot as "Michael Jordan Indians" because many are largely African-American by blood descent. This is not unusual in the New England states, where freed slaves often married native Americans in the nineteenth century. Black Pequot tribal member Joey Carter responded to Trump with a laugh: "You can call us anything you want, just call us at the bank."

Above: *Inside a Northeastern native-owned casino. The fortunes of Connecticut's Mashantucket Pequot have been altered the most dramatically by gaming. "Ours is a small tribe....We have survived, and now we flourish," commented one member. Another, Chris Pearson, said in a 1995 interview: "Native Americans are a very spiritual people and we don't have a love for gaming. We do, however, have a love for our families and that's what influenced our decision to build the casino."*

> *"Now we're on top and we're going to see that our people are taken care of."*
>
> —MICHAEL THOMAS, MASHANTUCKET PEQUOT

Other nations beside the Mashantucket Pequot have had financial success with gaming operations. These include the Menominee and Oneida of Wisconsin, the Agua Caliente Band of Cahuilla in California, the Coeur d'Alene in Idaho, and the Shakopee of Minnesota. Gaming has been good for tribes in that it has produced income where there was poverty before. It has put many tribes on the map financially, so that they need no longer beg for loans from the BIA or banks. It has also given many native Americans a sense of pride that they can achieve such economic success and proficiency at high finance. But it is no panacea, and the gaming era of the 1980s and 1990s has left most reservations where they were to begin with: poor.

Not all reservations are located to take advantage of gaming; tourism and demographic patterns have to be right. Nor do the leaders of more traditional native nations want gaming: the Navajo, among others, have refused to intro-duce it into their country. But the Mashantuckets and their fellow achievers take pride in their new-found wealth and power. Tribal Council member Michael Thomas stated:

The white man drove us into the swamp [in the 1630s] and we survived. Now we're on top and we're going to see that our people are taken care of.

Trouble Resurfacing

As in the United States, the native nations in Canada have never ceased asserting their rights and sovereignty, and in recent years standoffs with government forces have been occurring with increasing frequency.

In July 1990 the "Oka Crisis" began when police tried to dismantle a roadblock that Mohawks had set up to prevent municipal authorities from expanding a golf course onto land that the native population of Kanesatake, in Quebec, had claimed for thousands of years.

Right: *A scene of conflict during the Oka Crisis on Mohawk ancestral land, where plans for a golf-course extension resulted in the dispatch of Canadian soldiers.*

A 78-day standoff ensued, galvanizing native political activists across Canada. One Mohawk demonstrator said:

Their treaties, like our treaties, are being broken time and time again....There is still great anger here....The land is our identity, our life, and they wanted to take it away from us. Now they treat us like criminals. They call us murderers and thieves. Our land claims are not settled. Nothing is resolved.

During the spring and summer of 1995, flare-ups occurred from New Brunswick to British Columbia. In British Columbia, the Shuswap were attempting to conduct their tribal Sun Dance ceremony. Cowboys were angered when the Indians fenced in their sacred area, keeping cattle away from the holy tree. When the cowboys attacked, the Shuswap fought back. Canadian Mounties soon arrived in force.

The Shuswap, along with supporters from other nations including the Mohawk, were finally persuaded to surrender because their children refused to leave them during what they feared might be a final fight. In the courtroom, their non-native lawyer, Bruce Clark, was ruled out of order when he attempted to invoke the Royal Proclamation Act of 1763, under which native peoples still own most of British Columbia. This prompted former U.S. attorney general Ramsey Clark to write a letter of protest to the judge. In a stinging rebuke, he criticized the fact that those arrested were denied access to their attorney, deprived of their clothing, and brought into court wearing paper garments.

Their attorney was ordered to undergo a psychiatric evaluation to determine his competence. "Have you no sense of judicial ethics, or common decency?" Clark demanded in the letter. "You give the appearance of an arrogant and hateful tyrant....Do you expect Indian peoples to believe they can receive justice in your court? You should dismiss the contempt of court charges against Bruce Clark, cancel the unwarranted request for a psychiatric evaluation, order his immediate release and rescue yourself from further involvement in these cases."

By the 1990s, the growth of the worldwide human rights movements had served to pub-licize abuses against indigenous peoples and make such behavior unacceptable on the North American continent. Infringements and disputes may persist, but the naked abuses of civil rights have become a thing of the past. Discussions between Canadian politicians and Inuit leaders in 1991 confirmed the framework for Nunavut as a self-governing territory. In 1994 Bill Clinton convened a meeting with leaders of all federally recognized tribes to provide a forum for discussion. The bullet, it seems, has finally succumbed to more civilized methods of communication.

Above: *Negotiators attempt to bring the Oka Crisis to a peaceful, negotiated resolution.*

Little to Celebrate

The 500th anniversary of Columbus's landfall in 1492 was no cause for celebration among native Americans. As the anniversary drew near, many groups were outspoken in deploring the effects of European culture on the Americas. Millions had perished; entire cultures had been wiped out. As Seneca educator Stephanie Betancourt put it, "[For us,] these are days of mourning."

Despite the hoopla surrounding the event, many Americans came up with more appropriate ways to celebrate the anniversary. The city of Berkeley, California, declared Indigenous People's Day, and many other communities held sit-ins, teach-ins, and countermarches. Composer White Cloud Wolfhawk premiered his opera *Get Lost (Again) Columbus*. Schools reappraised the traditional presentation of Columbus as a hero and offered a more balanced point of view. For many native Americans, it became an empowering opportunity to tell the world: "Columbus Was Lost. We're Not."

Opposite: *Portrait of a proud nation.*

Completing The Sacred Circle

In 1990, one hundred years after the first massacre at Wounded Knee, leaders at Pine Ridge organized the Big Foot Memorial Ride. In the last week of December, Indian riders traversed the long snowy route traveled by Big Foot and his band. This time, the non-native supporters were the ones on foot. The event proved symbolic of history for native Americans completing a circle: the past was confronted and honored; from the lowest point in the First Nations' history, a century of rebirth and renewal had prevailed.

During the preparations for the memorial, *Indian Country Today*, the nation's largest native-owned newspaper, printed an exchange of letters that began with a moving account by Italian-American Gino Battista of his feelings after visiting the Rosebud and Pine Ridge reservations, where he had learned for the first time about the violent days of the past. "God forgive us for being so ignorant," he wrote:

The shame that we feel haunts us today. How can a country who boasts its greatness, turn its back on the very people who gave so much and asked for so little? …We are a people without roots and should kiss the ground you walk on for giving us a chance at a new way of life in a new land.

The average non-Indian has no idea of what Wounded Knee was. It's not in our history books, nor do the educators dwell on it….I cannot rest and have a clear conscience unless I try to do something, not just for myself but also for the government and the Lakota people to show there are non-Indians who care, and are aware of our government's wrongdoing.

Shortly after this letter was published, a surprised native American reader wrote in reply:

Most non-Indians come to South Dakota to see sites like Mount Rushmore…and they only come as tourists. This man came with an open mind and an honest heart….He has seen and felt the struggle we've been going through for some 120 years now. It's not very often you find a non-Indian admitting his people did wrong….I would like to tell this white brother he need not apologize for something he had no part of. What happened is in the past.

Thus began a correspondence and friendship between the two. Battista participated in the ride and arranged for a statue of Chief Big Foot to be commissioned for the ceremonies. Conger Beasley, Jr., an author and journalist, was another non-native participant in the observance. He described the procession and its culmination, a dance of celebration in which all were invited to participate:

I felt part of a living organism, absorbed in the currents of a mysterious emotion that was as powerful as anything I have ever experienced….Buoyed by the sound, transported by the high-pitched voices, the people in the two lines—myself happily among them—wove with elaborate courtesy in and out of one another's grasp, circling, circling. Circling.

Glossary of Tribes and Language Groups

Early sources rarely specify details of individual tribes and often contain inaccuracies. The following is a partial listing of North American native peoples by region and linguistic group.

ARCTIC/SUBARCTIC REGION
Eskaleut language group
Aleut
Inuit (Eskimo)
Athapaskan language group
Gwich'in
Yupik
Algonquian language group
Montagnais
Naskapi

NORTHEASTERN/ATLANTIC REGIONS
Algonquian language group
Abenaki
Cree
Delaware (Lenape)
Mahican
Micmac
Menominee
Montagnais
Narragansett
Ojibwa (Chippewa)
Ottawa
Penobscot
Powhatan
Potawatomi
Pequot
Sauk and Fox
Shawnee
Wampanoag
Iroquoian language group
Iroquois
    Cayuga
    Mohawk
    Oneida
    Onondaga
    Seneca
Tuscarora
Wyandot (Huron)

SOUTHEASTERN REGION
Muskogean language group
Chickasaw
Choctaw
Creek
Natchez
Seminole
Iroquoian language group
Cherokee

SOUTHWESTERN REGION
Tanoan language group (Puebloans)
Tewa
Yaqui
Numic language group
Hopi
Athapaskan language group
Apache
    Chiricahua
    Jicarilla
    Mescalero
    Mimbrano
    San Carlos
Navajo (Diné)
Penutian language group
Maidu
Miwok
Yokut
Zuñi
Hokan language group
Chumash
Havasupai
Mojave
Pomo
Yavapai
Piman language group
Pima
Papago

PLAINS and PLATEAU REGIONS
Algonquian language group
Arapaho
Blackfeet
Cheyenne
Gros Ventre
Plains Cree
Plains Ojibwa (Chippewa)
Penutian language group
Cayuse
Maidu
Modoc

Sioux/Siouan language group
Assiniboine
Crow
Dakota (Santee) Sioux
Hunkpapa Sioux
Lakota Sioux
Oglala Sioux
Omaha
Osage
Ponca
Winnebago
Nakota (Yankton) Sioux
Cadoan language group
Caddo
Pawnee
Wichita
Uto-Aztecan language group
Comanche
Kiowa
Paiute
Shoshone
Ute
Sahaptian language group
Nez Percé
Umatilla
Walla Walla
Yakima

NORTHWESTERN REGION
Na-dene language group
Athapaskan
Tlingit
Penutian language group
Chinook
Clackamas
Coosan
Tsimshian
Wishram
Salishan language group
Bella Coola
Couer d'Aléne
Dwamish
Haida
Quinault
Salish (Flathead)
Shuswap
Squamish
Wakashan language group
Kwakiutl
Makah
Nootka

Selected Bibliography and Sources

Sources, especially those transcribing oral histories, vary widely in styling, language, and attributed origin. The editors have selected what they believe to be the most authoritative text in cases where discrepancies arise.

Armstrong, Virginia Irving, comp. *I Have Spoken: American History Through the Voices of the Indians.* Swallow Press/Ohio Univ. Press, Athens. 1991.

Axtell, James. *The Invasion Within: The Contest of Cultures in Colonial North America.* Oxford University Press, New York, 1985.

Ballantine, Betty and Ian, eds. *The Native Americans: An Illustrated History.* Turner Publishing, Atlanta, 1993.

Bataille, Gretchen M., and Kathleen M. Sands. *American Indian Women: Telling Their Lives.* Univ. of Nebraska Press, Lincoln, 1984.

Berry, Thomas. *The Dream of the Earth.* Sierra Club Books, San Francisco, 1988.

Brady, Cyrus Townsend. *The Sioux Indian Wars: From the Powder River to the Little Big Horn.* Barnes & Noble, New York, 1992.

Brown, Dee. *Bury My Heart at Wounded Knee: An Indian History of the American West.* Henry Holt and Co., New York, 1991.

Carlson, Vada F., ed. and comp. *No Turning Back.* Univ. of New Mexico Press, Albuquerque, 1964.

Clark, Bruce. *Native Liberty, Crown Sovereignty: The Existing Aboriginal Right of Self-Government in Canada.* McGill-Queen's University Press, Montreal, 1992.

Dana, Richard Henry, Jr. *Two Years Before the Mast.* Penguin Books USA, New York, 1964.

Deloria, Vine Jr. *Custer Died for Your Sins: An Indian Manifesto.* Univ. of Oklahoma Press, Norman, 1989.

DeMallie, Raymond J., ed. *The Sixth Grandfather: Black Elk's Teachings, Given to John G. Neihardt.* Univ. of Nebraska Press, Lincoln, 1984.

Dickens, Charles. *American Notes for General Circulation.* Penguin Books Ltd., London, 1986.

Erdoes, Richard, and Alfonso Ortiz, eds. *American Indian Myths and Legends.* Pantheon Books, New York, 1984.

Espinosa, J. Manuel, ed. *The Pueblo Indian Revolt of 1696 and the Franciscan Missions in New Mexico: Letters of the Missionaries and Related Documents.* Univ. of Oklahoma Press, Norman, 1988.

Farley, Ronnie. *Women of the Native Struggle.* Orion Books. The Library of the American Indian series, New York, 1993.

Fischer, David Hackett. *Albion's Seed: Four British Folkways in America.* Oxford Univ. Press, New York, 1989.

Foreman, Grant. *Indian Removal: The Emigration of the Five Civilized Tribes of Indians.* Univ. of Oklahoma Press. 1989.

Garcilaso de la Vega (El Inca). *Royal Commentaries of the Incas, and General History of Peru, I and II.* University of Texas Press, Austin, 1966.

Green, Rayna. *Women in American Indian Society.* Chelsea House, New York, 1992.

Greenblatt, Stephen, ed. *New World Encounters.* Univ. of California Press, Los Angeles, 1993.

Hill, Tom, and Richard W. Hill, eds. *Creation's Journey: Native American Identity and Belief.* Smithsonian Institution Press, Washington, D.C., 1994.

Hirschfelder, Arlene, ed. *Native Heritage: Personal Accounts by American Indians, 1790 to the Present.* Macmillan, New York, 1995.

Jackson, Helen. *A Century of Dishonor.* Barnes & Noble, New York, 1993.

Jennings, Francis. *The Invasion of America: Indians, Colonialism, and the Cant of Conquest.* W.W. Norton, New York, 1976.

Johnson-Tekahionwake, E. Pauline. *Legends of Vancouver.* Quarry Press, Kingston, Ontario, 1991.

Josephy, Alvin M., Jr. *500 Nations: An Illustrated History of North American Indians.* Alfred A. Knopf, New York, 1994.

Krupat, Arnold, ed. *Native American Autobiography: An Anthology.* Univ. of Wisconsin Press, Madison, 1994.

Linderman, Frank B. *Pretty-shield, Medicine Woman of the Crows.* Univ. of Nebraska Press, Lincoln, 1972.

Lyons, Oren R., and John C. Mohawk, eds. *Exiled in the Land of the Free: Democracy, Indian Nations, and the U.S. Constitution.* Clear Light Publishers, Santa Fe, 1992.

Mails, Thomas E. *Fools Crow.* Univ. of Nebraska Press, Lincoln, 1993.

Matthiessen, Peter. *In The Spirit of Crazy Horse.* Penguin Books USA, New York, 1992.

McCallum, James Dow, ed. *The Letters of Eleazar Wheelock's Indians.* Dartmouth College Ms. Series No. 1, Dartmouth College Pubns., Hanover, N.H., 1932.

McGregor, James H. *The Wounded Knee Massacre: From the Viewpoint of the Sioux.* Fensky Printing, Inc., Rapid City, S.D., 1987.

Means, Russell. *Where White Men Fear to Tread.* St. Martin's Press, New York, 1995.

Morton, Desmond. *A Short History of Canada.* McClelland and Stewart Inc., Toronto, 1994.

Nabokov, Peter, ed. *Native American Testimony: A Chronicle of Indian-White Relations from Prophecy to the Present.* Penguin Books USA, New York, 1992.

Neihardt, John G., comp. *Black Elk Speaks.* Univ. of Nebraska Press, Lincoln, 1990.

Ortiz, Alfonso, ed. *New Perspectives on the Pueblos.* Univ. of New Mexico Press, Albuquerque, 1972.

Parabola: The Magazine of Myth and Tradition. Winter 1993 and 1994.

Peavy, Linda, and Ursula Smith. *Pioneer Women: The Lives of Women on the Frontier.* Saraband Inc., Rowayton, Conn., 1996.

Sandoz, Mari. *These Were the Sioux.* Univ. of Nebraska Press, Lincoln, 1985.

Seaver, James E. *A Narrative of the Life of Mrs. Mary Jemison.* Syracuse Univ. Press, Syracuse, 1990.

"Some Transactions between the Indians and Friends in Pennsylvania, in 1791 & 1792." Swarthmore College Quaker Collection, courtesy the Clement M. Biddle Fund, 1924.

Spencer, O.M. *The Indian Captivity of O.M. Spencer.* Dover Pubns., New York, 1995.

Standing Bear, Luther. *Land of the Spotted Eagle.* Univ. of Nebraska Press, Lincoln, 1978.

Steer, Diana. *Native American Women.* Barnes & Noble, New York, 1996.

Stockel, H. Henrietta. *Women of the Apache Nation: Voices of Truth.* Univ. of Nevada Press, Reno, 1991.

Suzuki, David, and Peter Knudtson. *Wisdom of the Elders: Honoring Sacred Native Visions of Nature.* Bantam Books, New York, 1992.

Tanner, Ogden. *The Canadians (The Old West Series).* Time-Life Books, New York, 1977.

Taylor, Colin. *Myths of the North American Indians.* Barnes & Noble, New York, 1995.

Udall, Louise, ed. and comp. *Me and Mine: The Life Story of Helen Sekaquaptewa.* Univ. of Arizona Press, Tucson, 1985.

Utley, Robert M. *The Lance and the Shield: The Life and Times of Sitting Bull.* Henry Holt and Co., New York, 1993.

Vanderwerth, W.C., comp. *Indian Oratory: Famous Speeches by Noted Indian Chieftains.* Univ. of Oklahoma Press, Norman, 1971.

Viola, Herman, J. *After Columbus: The Smithsonian Chronicle of the North American Indians.* Orion Books, New York, 1990.

Wall, Steve, and Harvey Arden. *Wisdomkeepers: Meetings with Native American Spiritual Elders.* Beyond Words Publishing, Portland, 1990.

Weatherford, Jack. *Indian Givers: How the Indians of the Americas Transformed the World.* Fawcett Pubns., New York, 1988.

———. *Native Roots: How the Indians Enriched America.* Fawcett Pubns., New York, 1991.

Woodhead, Henry, ed. *The American Indians Series.* Time-Life Books, New York, 1992–96.

Woodward, Meredith Bain. *Land of Dreams: A History in Photographs of the British Columbia Interior.* Altitude Publishing, Vancouver, 1993.

Wright, Ronald. *Stolen Continents: The "New World" Through Indian Eyes.* Houghton Mifflin, New York, 1992.

Index

Acknowledgements

The publisher would like to thank the following individuals for their assistance in the preparation of this book: Emily Elizabeth Head, Robin Langley Sommer. Grateful acknowledgement is also made to the following individuals and institutions for permission to reproduce photographs:
Berninghaus Family Collection: 141; © **Carla Breeze:** 178b; **Corbis-Bettmann:** 6, 19, 22t, 23t, 27 (both), 34, 35, 36, 39 (both), 43 (both), 47t, 51, 54, 55t, 62b, 67b, 71, 73t, 75 (both), 78b, 82, 83b, 86, 87t & b, 88b, 91b, 97t, 100, 101, 107, 108, 109 (both), 113b, 115b, 118, 119, 122, 124, 125, 126, 132b, 134, 135, 138, 139, 140t & b, 143 (all), 146 (both), 147 (both), 150 (both), 152t, 153, 164b; **CorelDraw:** 58, 70b, 112, 136-7; **Cumberland County Historical Society, Carlisle, PA:** 102, 103; **The Field Museum, Chicago:** 94b (neg # 9511); © **Rachel Hunt:** 38; **Library of Congress:** 2, 4, 8, 9, 10, 11, 12, 13, 14, 15, 16, 17, 18 (both), 20, 21 (both), 22b, 23b, 24, 25 (both), 26, 28, 29, 30, 31 (both), 32, 33, 40, 41, 44, 45, 48t, 52–3, 53b, 55b, 56, 57, 59 (both), 60, 61 (both), 62t, 63 (both), 64, 65, 66, 67t, 68, 69, 70t, 72t, 76, 77, 80, 81, 83t, 84, 93, 94t, 98, 97b, 106, 110, 114, 115t, 120, 128, 129, 133, 142; **Montana Historical Society, Helena:** 123; **Museum of New Mexico:** 126 (photo by T. Harmon Parkhurst, neg # 12505); **National Archives:** 42, 96, 99 (both), 113t; **National Archives of Canada:** 46, 47b, 49, 50 (both), 89, 90, 91t, 92, 121; **Ness Collection/Corbis-Bettmann:** 117; **Nevada State Museum:** 132t; **Planet Art:** 72b, 74, 78t, 80, 87l, 95, 111; **Reuters/Corbis-Bettmann:** 154, 166t, 171t, 173t; **South Dakota State Historical Society:** 116; © **Michael Tincher:** 178t, 179 (both); **The University Museum, University of Pennsylvania:** 149b (neg # G6-11673); **UPI/Corbis-Bettmann:** 110, 130 (both), 131, 144b, 145 (both), 148t, 149t, 152b, 155, 156 (both), 157 (both), 158, 159, 160 (both), 161, 162, 163, 164t, 165 (both), 166b, 167, 168 (both), 169 (both), 170, 171b, 172 (all), 173b, 174, 175, 176 (both), 180, 181, 182, 183; **USMA Library, West Point, NY:** 104 (both), 105 (both) [John Gregory Bourke Collection]; **Wyoming State Museum, Division of Cultural Resources:** 73b; © **Charles Ziga:** 140 left, 144t.